SCHOLASTIC

READ&RESP▼ND

Bringing the best books to life in the classroom

Guided Reading

Key Stage 1

Comprehensive guided reading notes for:

- **Jasper's Beanstalk**
- **Owl Babies**
- **We're Going on a Bear Hunt**
- **Zog**
- **Handa's Surprise**
- **Superworm**

AGES 5–6

Scholastic Education, an imprint of Scholastic Ltd
Book End, Range Road, Witney, Oxfordshire, OX29 0YD
Registered office: Westfield Road, Southam, Warwickshire CV47 0RA
www.scholastic.co.uk
© 2017, Scholastic Ltd
1 2 3 4 5 6 7 8 9   7 8 9 0 1 2 3 4 5 6

British Library Cataloguing-in-Publication Data
A catalogue record for this book is available from the British Library.
ISBN 978-1407-16945-3
Printed and bound by Ashford Colour Press

Due to the nature of the web we cannot guarantee the content or links of any site mentioned. We strongly recommend that teachers check websites before using them in the classroom.

Every effort has been made to trace copyright holders for the works reproduced in this book, and the publishers apologise for any inadvertent omissions.

Extracts from National Curriculum for England, English Programme of Study © Crown Copyright. Reproduced under the terms of the Open Government Licence (OGL). www.nationalarchives.gov.uk/doc/open-government-licence/version/3/

Authors Jean Evans and Samantha Pope
Editorial Rachel Morgan, Jenny Wilcox, Kate Buckley, Niamh O'Carroll, Jennie Clifford
Cover and Series Design Neil Salt and Nicolle Thomas
Layout Neil Salt

CONTENTS

▼ INTRODUCTION

Read & Respond provides teaching ideas related to a specific children's book. The series focuses on best-loved books and brings you ways to use them to engage your class and enthuse them about reading. This book provides detailed guided reading sessions for six children's books.

GUIDED READING

Guided reading is usually conducted in small groups with children of a similar reading ability, under teacher guidance. The groups are often around six to eight children, although may be fewer depending on the children in your class. The sessions are likely to be short, around 20 minutes, and focused on reading and comprehension skills.

There should be one focus text and each child should have a copy of it. The text should be slightly more challenging than the children's independent reading level, where they can read and understand the vast majority of the text independently. The teacher facilitation of guided reading allows for the children to access more challenging materials in a supported environment – they should still be able to understand and access 90 per cent of the content though.

Guided reading is much more than just reading in turns. Time should be given for reading independently; the teacher may wish to listen to individual children, but this should be followed up by checking the children's understanding and comprehension of the text through discussion and questioning.

How this book relates to the *Read & Respond* teacher's book

This book can be used for stand-alone sessions or in conjunction with the corresponding *Read & Respond* teacher's books. Each *Read & Respond* teacher's book is designed for whole-class teaching and contains a variety of activities that look at punctuation, phonics and spelling; plot, character and setting; speaking and listening; and writing.

While there are guided reading notes in the teacher's book, the ones provided in this book are much more detailed and therefore the two books can work together. If you are using a carousel system for guided reading, then the teacher's book may provide supporting activities to use when the children are not in the guided reading group. Within this book, there may be some optional links referenced to the *Read & Respond* teacher's book, where work could be expanded.

ABOUT THE BOOK

Each children's book has been divided into four guided reading sessions. The sessions work through each book progressively, so you read it over a number of weeks. It has been assumed that the sessions will be conducted in guided reading groups of around six to eight children; if you plan to use them differently, then they can be adapted accordingly. Each session follows a similar structure:

Session aims: The purpose of the session and what children will be focused on in their reading.

Before the session: If there is anything the children need to do prior to the session, such as reading some of the book, this will be identified here.

Read: This section will focus on the children reading the text either independently or as a group. It may be reading new chapters or sections of the book or re-reading parts of the book that they have read previously. They should consider questions about the text while reading and then discuss these as a group to check their understanding.

Revisit and respond: A range of different activities will have been provided under this heading to provide flexibility to select appropriate tasks for the group. As each session is only intended to be around 20 minutes long, it is advised that one or two of these activity ideas are used to meet the needs of your children.

Assessment opportunities: A bank of questions has been provided which could be used at any point in the session as relevant. They are sub-divided into headings to identify the purpose of the type of question.

At the end of the book, you will find two templates that you can use to support your guided reading sessions:

Guided Reading Bookmark Template: This template provides a bookmark that you can complete and give to the children as reference. It could include the questions you want them to consider when reading or you could use the assessment opportunities questions for the children to discuss.

Guided Reading Record Template: A template to record any notes from a guided reading session so you have a record that you can refer to.

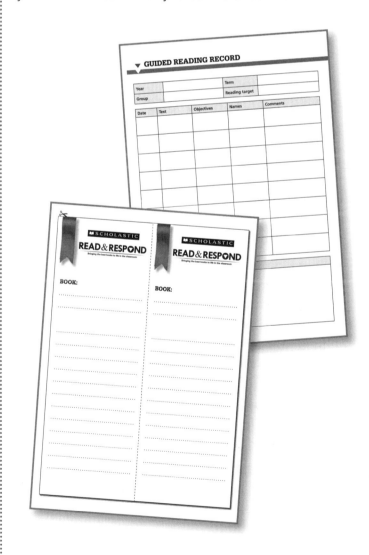

SESSION 1: JASPER'S BEAN

SESSION AIMS

Discuss the significance of the title and events; predict what might happen.

READ

- Ask the children to read the first three spreads independently. Invite them to consider some of these questions.
  - Who do you think this story is about? Why?
  - Where is Jasper?
  - Name the days mentioned. What can you say about the order in which they occur?
  - What does Jasper do on each day?
  - What do you think he will do next? On what day will this happen?

During reading

- Move around the group and 'tune in' to hear children reading. Praise individuals for clarity.

REVISIT AND RESPOND

Bring the group back together and discuss some of the points below, which explore the cover, inner pages and first three spreads.

Note: Since there are only 20 minutes for each session, you are advised to focus on only one or two of the elements that are listed below.

- Draw attention to the names of the author and illustrator on the cover. Recall titles the children may be familiar with written by Nick Butterworth, particularly the *Percy the Park Keeper* books, and those written and illustrated by Mick Inkpen, such as *Kipper* and *Wibbly Pig*. Ask: *What did you like about these books? Who are the main characters? Do you think the characters and illustrations in this book will be similar? Do you think 'Inkpen' is a good name for an author or illustrator?*

- Read the title and explore the cover illustrations together. Depending on the edition, ask: *Who is this book about? What do you think Jasper likes doing? What do you think he is planning to do with all the tools? What sort of tools are they?* Read the short blurb on the back cover together, supporting children with unfamiliar words. Discuss the meaning of 'In spite of all the attention he lavishes on it'. Ask: *What sort of attention would you give to a bean you were trying to grow?*

- Depending on the edition, turn to the inner page and read the words 'This book belongs to:' together. Talk about the purpose of this page and the need for the dotted line. (It is for the owner to write their name on.) Explore the image of Jasper below and the book he is reading. Ask: *What is the title of Jasper's book? What is it about? What do you think Jasper might like about this book? What do you think the robin is pointing at?*

- Talk about what Jasper is doing on each of the first three spreads. Ask: *Can you find the verbs (doing words) that tell us this? What do you notice about the verbs 'planted' and 'watered'?* (They both end in 'ed'.) Recall that most verbs have this ending when we talk about actions that happen in the past. *Which is the other verb in this section?* ('found'.)

- Discuss the sequence of events that Jasper follows in his garden. Ask: *How often does Jasper do something in his garden? What happens on Monday? When does he plant the bean? When does he water it? If he follows his routine, which day do you think he will do something else in the garden? Why do you think it is good to have a sequence to follow?*

- Explore the illustrations on spreads 1 to 3 and discuss the additional information they provide. Ask: *Can you describe the bean? Can you explain how Jasper planted it? What did he do first? What tools did he use? What do you think he needs a stick for? Where did Jasper get the water from to water his bean? Have you ever used a garden tap? What does Jasper use to pour water onto his bean? What does the expression on Jasper's face tell us about how he feels about planting and caring for his bean?*

- Recall the rules for using capital letters at the start of sentences, for names and for the days of the week. Ask pairs to find examples of capitals used for these reasons in this section.
- Discuss the text and layout. Ask: *Why do you think the print is so large? Is there a pattern to the way the text and illustrations are arranged on the pages?* (The illustrations are on the page opposite the text.)

Ask the children to revisit the text and illustrations to support their answers. Encourage them to read aloud back to the group when quoting from the text.

ASSESSMENT OPPORTUNITIES

The following bank of question prompts provides a quick and easy means of monitoring the children's comprehension skills and understanding of the text. The children's answers to a question must be supported by evidence from the text.

Understanding
- What type of animal is the main character?
- Which garden creature comes to watch Jasper?

Inferences
- What do you think Jasper was hoping for when he planted the bean? What makes you think this?
- What book title does this one remind you of? What events in the story do you think might be similar?

Predicting
- What do you think Jasper still needs to do to make sure his beanstalk grows?
- Do you think any other characters will come into the story as you read on?

Main ideas
- What is the first thing Jasper needed to do with his bean?
- What would happen if Jasper did not water his bean?
- Do you think this book is written for early or experienced readers? Why do you think this?

Language, structure and presentation
- Which words start with a capital letter in this section, and why?
- What do the sentences on each page have in common? Which word appears in all of them?

Themes and conventions
- Is this a fiction or non-fiction book? How do you know?
- What do you think the type of story is from the title and illustration on the cover? (Fantasy/fairy tale/funny tale.)

SESSION 2: JASPER THE GARDENER

SESSION AIMS

Identify the main character and setting; predict what might happen.

READ

- Ask the children to read spreads 4, 5 and 6 independently, considering some of these questions.
    - Can you name the days mentioned in this section? Which day has not been mentioned yet?
    - Why did Jasper go outside on Friday night instead of during the day?
    - What did Jasper do on Saturday?
    - What do you think will happen next, and when?

During reading

- Move around the group and 'tune in' to hear individuals read aloud. Encourage and praise good expression.

REVISIT AND RESPOND

Bring the group back together and discuss some of the points below.

Note: Since there are only 20 minutes for each session, you are advised to focus on only one or two of the elements that are listed below.

- Discuss Jasper's actions on spreads 4 to 6 and ask: *Which was Jasper's busiest day? Why did he do so many things on this day? Has the bean started growing yet? How would you feel if you were waiting for something to grow and there was no sign? Do you think Jasper is impatient and trying everything he can to make his bean grow more quickly? Have you ever felt impatient? Can you describe this feeling?*

- Ask the children to name as many of Jasper's tools as they can (rake, hoe, spade, sprayer, mower), and explain how to use each one. Name any that the children are unfamiliar with and explain their use. Then ask the children to work in pairs to make up a simple sentence about how each tool is used. (Give an example using a different tool, such as 'Clippers are used to cut hedges and bushes'.)

- Explore the illustration of Jasper using the mower. Ask: *Where have you seen this picture before?* (On the back cover – this may depend on the edition.) *What is a mower used for? Can you see any grass in the picture? Why is Jasper using a mower on the soil?* (If children do not suggest a reason, recall the discussion about his impatience leading to him trying everything.) *What has Jasper chopped up with the mower?* (The stick.) *Do you think he meant to? Do you think he realises he has done this? How will he know where he has planted his bean now? What could he do about his mistake?*

- Ask the children where the illustration on spread 4 is repeated. (On the front cover – this may depend on the edition.) Compare the two illustrations. Ask: *Are they exactly the same? What is different about them?* (The hose is wound around the hoe in one picture.) *Why do you think the author and illustrator chose this particular picture to put on the cover? What does it tell us about the story inside?*

- Discuss the illustration on spread 5. Ask: *Why does Jasper need a torch? How can you tell it is night-time? Why is he collecting slugs and snails? What do you think he will do with them? What is he carrying the slugs and snails in?*

- Recall previous discussion about the 'ed' endings of verbs indicating that these actions happened in the past. Ask the children to find the verbs ending in 'ed' in this section. Talk about the irregular verb form 'dug' on spread 4.

- Explore the illustrations and discuss the additional information they provide. Ask: *Which days did the robin watch Jasper while he was busy? Where do you think the robin was on Friday night? Why do you think robins like to watch gardeners?* (They are waiting for insects and grubs to eat.) *Do you think Jasper will catch more snails or more slugs? What makes you think this?* Recall talking about Jasper's expression in the first section. *Has his expression changed at all in this part of the story? What does this tell us about Jasper's usual mood and personality?*

- Discuss the text and layout. Ask: *What is different about the way the text and illustration appear on spread 5? Why do you think the picture is stretched across both pages with the text running along the bottom?* (To show the distance Jasper searched.)

Ask the children to revisit the text and illustrations to support their answers. Encourage them to read aloud back to the group when quoting from the text.

ASSESSMENT OPPORTUNITIES

The following bank of question prompts provides a quick and easy means of monitoring the children's comprehension skills and understanding of the text. The children's answers to a question must be supported by evidence from the text.

Understanding

- Which bird is often called 'the gardener's friend' because it likes watching gardeners and waiting for insects and grubs to appear?
- Which of Jasper's tools would you use to make a hole in the ground/smooth out the soil/break up lumps and bumps in the soil/spray liquid onto a plant/cut the grass?

Inferences

- Why will it be difficult for Jasper to remember where he has planted his bean after the end of this section?
- What do you like about Jasper? What sort of things would you do together?

Predicting

- Do you think the bean will grow any faster with the extra attention Jasper gives to it?
- What do you think will happen next?

Main ideas

- When do slugs and snails like to come out into the garden? What other creatures like to come out at night?
- How do you think Jasper will feel if the bean does not grow? Do you think he will grow another bean?

Language, structure and presentation

- Which connecting word does the author use to join the verbs in the first sentence on spread 4?

- What do the sentences on each page have in common? Which word appears in all of them?

Themes and conventions

- Do you think this is a funny story? What makes you laugh in this section?
- What did you like best about this part of the story?

SESSION 3: WHERE'S MY BEAN?

Link what they read or listen to with their own experiences.

READ

- Ask the children to read the next three spreads (7 to 9) independently. Invite them to consider some of these questions.
  - Can you name the days mentioned? Which day is repeated from the first section? Which new garden tool does Jasper use? (Garden hose.)
  - What did Jasper do on Sunday? What was he waiting for?
  - When did he dig the bean up again? Why did he do this?
  - How and why has Jasper's mood changed in this part of the story?
  - What do you think will happen next? Will Jasper ever grow his beanstalk?

During reading

- Move around the group listening in as children are reading. Praise individuals for clarity.

REVISIT AND RESPOND

Bring the group back together and discuss some of the points below.

Note: Since there are only 20 minutes for each session, you are advised to focus on only one or two of the elements that are listed below.

- Discuss the time span of the story so far. Ask: *How do you know that eight days have passed since Jasper found the bean?* Compare the appearance of the bean when Jasper planted it with how it looks when he digs it up again. Ask: *Has it changed at all? Has it started to grow?*
- Talk about Jasper's changing mood during this section. Ask: *How can you tell that Jasper is not as happy now? How would you describe his mood? How has his expression changed? What has happened to his mouth? How do his ears and*

whiskers reflect his mood? (Drooping ears, wiggling whiskers.) Encourage children to compare these signs with their own appearance when they are sad. Ask whether their mouths turn down and their shoulders droop. Talk about things that make them feel like this.

- Focus on spread 7. Recall the connecting word 'and' used to join the list of actions in the last section. Ask: *Which verb does the author repeat three times on this page?* Point out the 'ed' endings for the verbs and ask: *What does this ending tell us about when this happened? What is the connecting word used to join these verbs? Why do you think the author has used this repetition?* (To emphasise what a long wait Jasper was having.) Recall the use of an ellipsis, or explain this if the children are unfamiliar. Ask: *Why do you think the author would like the reader to pause at the end of this page? Do you think Jasper's wish will come true and the bean will be growing when you turn the page?*

- Look at the illustration on the next spread and read the text together. Ask: *Were you correct about what would happen next? What is Jasper doing? Look at the soil and worms flying through the air. What does this tell you about the way Jasper is digging? What do you think his mood is now – angry, excited, worried, sad, happy, frantic? What do you think the bean will be like when he finds it?*

- Draw attention to the inverted commas on spread 9, explaining their use if necessary. Ask the children to read Jasper's words together. Now discuss the illustration of Jasper. Talk about how sad he looks and discuss how we sometimes change our voices when we feel sad. Ask the children to read Jasper's words again in sad voices.

- Recall the story of 'Jack and the Beanstalk' and discuss what happened to Jack's beans when he threw them on the ground. What do the children think will happen to Jasper's bean when it lands on the ground?

- Explore the actions of the robin. Notice how it watches Jasper's frantic digging with interest and then hops onto Jasper's foot when he is sitting on the ground looking glum. Ask: *Do you think the robin is trying to cheer Jasper up? Do you do this if you have a friend who is feeling sad? How do you think a robin could cheer up a sad cat?* (Perhaps it could sing a song.)

Ask the children to revisit the text and illustrations to support their answers. Encourage them to read aloud back to the group when quoting from the text.

ASSESSMENT OPPORTUNITIES

The following bank of question prompts provides a quick and easy means of monitoring the children's comprehension skills and understanding of the text. The children's answers to a question must be supported by evidence from the text.

Understanding

- Jasper found his bean on a Monday. What happened exactly a week later?
- Why did Jasper throw the bean away? What did he say about it?

Inferences

- Do you think Jasper is patient or impatient on the first spread of this part of the story? Which repeated word tells you this?
- Do you think Jasper is patient or impatient on the second spread? Did the illustration affect the way you answered this?

Predicting

- Do you think that Jasper's words are true: that the bean will never make a beanstalk?
- What do you think will happen in the last section? How do you think the story will end?

Main ideas

- How did the robin show that he was Jasper's friend?
- Why does Jasper think the bean will never make a beanstalk?

Language, structure and presentation

- Can you find any patterns in the text so far? What word does every sentence start with for the first seven spreads? How does this change on spread 8?

Themes and conventions

- Do you think this section is as funny as the others? Does anything make you laugh in it? What makes you sad in this section?
- So far there has been just one sentence in large print on every page. Who do you think would like to read this book?

▼ SESSION 4: WORTH WAITING FOR

SESSION AIMS

Discuss the significance of the title and events.

READ

- Ask the children to read the last three spreads (10 to 12) independently, bearing in mind some of these questions.
    - How would you describe the amount of time that passes in this last section? Which day is the only one mentioned?
    - How do the illustrations on spread 10 show that time is passing? Which repeated word describes the time?
    - What was Jasper waiting for before? Did he get what he wanted?
    - Why is Jasper looking for giants when the story ends?
    - What do you think he will do next?

During reading

- Move around the group and 'tune in' to hear children read. Praise individuals for clarity and expression.

REVISIT AND RESPOND

Bring the group back together and discuss some of the points below.

Note: Since there are only 20 minutes for each session, you are advised to focus on only one or two of the elements that are listed below.

- Discuss the illustrations and text on spread 10. Ask: *How many times has the author repeated the word 'long'? Why do you think he has done this? What other word tells you that time has passed?* ('later') *What was happening during this 'long, long, long' time? Do you think Jasper knew that the beanstalk was growing? What makes you think this? Who has noticed that the beanstalk has grown?*

- Draw attention to the ellipsis at the end of spread 10, reminding the group of its purpose, if necessary. Read the text and ask: *Why do you think the author wants the reader to pause before turning this page? Do you think there will be a surprise? What do you think this will be?*

- Turn the page and read the words 'It did!' together. Ask: *What do these important words tell us?* Explore the illustration and ask: *What is the robin pointing at? When have you discussed this illustration before?* (Possibly in the first session.) *Did you notice that the robin was pointing to something then? What is he trying to tell Jasper? When Jasper does see the beanstalk, what do you think he will want to do?*

- Discuss the purpose of brackets (to provide additional information) and then read the words inside brackets on this spread. Ask: *What extra information is given? Why do you think the letters are smaller than those above? Do you think it is to show the importance of the words above, or are the words in brackets simply the author thinking aloud? How would you read these words?* (Quietly and thoughtfully.) Now read the whole spread together again, changing volume and expression to suit the punctuation.

- Explore the final spread together and discuss the significance of the exclamation mark at the end of the sentence. (To emphasise strongly.) Read the text together with this emphasis. Ask: *Why is Jasper looking for giants? Which story does the beanstalk remind him of? What happened in that story?* Look at the illustration alongside and ask: *Do you think Jasper looks as if he is thinking as he strokes his whiskers? What might he be thinking? Will he try to climb up the beanstalk? What do you think will happen next?*

- Discuss how there are few adjectives to describe the characters and objects in this story, and so readers turn to the illustrations for this information. Talk about what the children know about Jasper, the robin and the beanstalk from the illustrations.

- Now that the children have read the entire story, discuss their opinions of it. Ask: *What is your favourite part of this story? What did you think of the main character? How would you describe him?*

Ask the children to revisit the text and illustrations to support their answers. Encourage them to read aloud back to the group when quoting from the text.

ASSESSMENT OPPORTUNITIES

The following bank of question prompts provides a quick and easy means of monitoring the children's comprehension skills and understanding of the text. The children's answers to a question must be supported by evidence from the text.

Understanding
- What happens in this part of the story?
- What is Jasper doing when the robin tries to attract his attention?
- If you could ask the robin a question about his actions, what would it be?

Inferences
- How do you think Jasper feels when he spots the beanstalk outside of the window?
- What do you think Jasper likes best about the story of 'Jack and the Beanstalk'? Why do you think this?

Predicting
- Was your prediction correct about what would be on the next page after you paused at the ellipsis?
- If you could climb Jasper's beanstalk, what do you think you would find at the top?
- Can you think of a different way to end the story?

Main ideas
- Why is this story called *Jasper's Beanstalk*? Which traditional tale is it linked to?
- Do you think this story carries a message? (Help children with this concept, if necessary, by discussing whether it is right to be impatient while waiting for something to happen, or better to wait patiently.) Who is impatient in this story? Do you think Jasper learns to be patient by the end of the story?

Language, structure and presentation
- Why do you think the words 'It did!' are printed in bold, large letters with an exclamation mark after them? How should you read these words?
- What is an adjective? Can you think of adjectives of your own to describe Jasper, the robin and the beanstalk?

Themes and conventions
- What did you think of the way that the story ends? Does it end as you expected? Would you have liked it to continue so you could find out what would happen after Jasper climbed the beanstalk?
- If the author wrote a book to follow this one (a sequel), what do you think it would be about?

SESSION 1: WHERE'S MUMMY?

SESSION AIMS

Make inferences on the basis of what is being said and done; predict what might happen.

READ

- Ask the children to read the first three spreads independently. Invite them to consider some of these questions.
  - Do you think there is one main character in this story or several? Why do you think that?
  - What are the names of the baby owls and their mother?
  - Where is this section of the story set? How do you know?
  - What happens in this section?
  - Where do the owls think that their mother has gone?
  - What do you think will happen next?

During reading

- While the group are reading, praise individuals for their clarity and for varying expression – for example, when characters are speaking.

REVISIT AND RESPOND

Bring the group back together and discuss some of the points below, which explore the cover and the first three spreads.

Note: Since there are only 20 minutes for each session, you are advised to focus on only one or two of the elements that are listed below.

- Read the title and explore the front cover illustration together. Ask: *Who is this book about? What makes you think this? What do you think might happen to these characters?* Read the first paragraph on the back cover together and consider this additional information. Ask: *What do we know about Owl Mother?* (She is not at home.) *What are the baby owls doing?*

- Explore the illustration of the owl 'house' on the first spread and ask children to describe it. Suggest that they use words from the text in their description. Ask: *What does the text tell us about where the house is, and the way it is constructed? What natural materials have the owls used to make their house comfortable? What word do we usually use for a bird's house? Why do you think the author has called the owls' nest their 'house'? Why do you think owls build their houses in holes in trees?*

- Focus on the images of the adult Owl Mother and her babies on the first spread. Ask: *Who do you think the large owl is? How do you know this? Describe the appearance of the baby owls. Do the baby feathers look the same as adult feathers?* Ask pairs to work together to find features the baby owls have in common with their mother. (They all have round brown eyes, sharp pointed beaks, feathers.)

- Find the inverted commas on spreads 2 and 3, and identify which owl is speaking. Talk about the reason for the question mark or exclamation mark after each owl speaks. Discuss how these words should be read, with the voice rising at the end of a question or emphasising the words before an exclamation mark. Try reading one spoken sentence at a time, each with appropriate emphasis. Now discuss how to create interesting voices for each character. Talk about how Sarah is the confident owl who asks important questions, Percy is the one who tries to sound brave but worries a lot, and Bill is the baby who just wants his mummy! Ask the children to practise these voices before reading the section again, choosing individuals to read the words of the characters. Repeat this with different children and discuss the best interpretation.

- Further investigate punctuation. Recall the use of brackets to give additional information, or explain this if necessary. Find the brackets on spread 3 and discuss why the author has used them. Draw attention to the use of italics for the word 'thought' immediately preceding the brackets. Explain that italics give emphasis to important words. Ask: *Why do you think the author is drawing our attention to the fact that the baby owls 'thought'? Would you expect owls to think? Does the information in brackets help to emphasise this information as well? Have you ever read about a 'wise owl'? Do you think that a wise creature would think about things a lot?*

- Return to the owl discussion and ask: *Which owl repeats his words? Why do you think he does this? What does he say? Do you think this repetition helps to emphasise how much he misses his mummy?* Being sensitive to individual circumstances, you could ask: *Have you ever missed someone when they have gone away? Can you describe this feeling?*

Ask the children to revisit the text and illustrations to support their answers. Encourage them to read quotes aloud to the rest of the group.

ASSESSMENT OPPORTUNITIES

The following bank of question prompts provides a quick and easy means of monitoring the children's comprehension skills and understanding of the text. The children's answers to a question must be supported by evidence from the text.

Understanding

- What type of birds are the main characters?
- What was the first thing they noticed when they woke up one night?

Inferences

- How did the babies feel when they discovered their mother had gone?
- Do you think the owl babies are safe inside their house? Why do you think this?

Predicting

- Do you think the Owl Mother will come back? What makes you think this?
- What do you think the babies will do while they are waiting for their mother to return?

Main ideas

- Why are the babies all alone in their house?
- Where do you think the Owl Mother has gone? What might she be doing?

Language, structure and presentation

- Can you find examples of capital letters used for names in this section?
- Which word has the author written in capitals? Why is 'GONE' such an important word in the sentence?

Themes and conventions

- What is the story language used in the opening sentence? ('Once there were'.)
- Is this a fiction or non-fiction book? How do you know?
- Why do you think the print is written in a light colour instead of black, which is used in most books? Do you like how the text looks?

▼ SESSION 2: BRANCH CONVERSATION

SESSION AIMS

Participate actively in collaborative conversations.

READ

- Ask the children to read spreads 4, 5 and 6 independently. Invite them to consider some of these questions.
  - Where do the baby owls wait for Owl Mother?
  - Why do you think they wait outside of their house instead of inside?
  - How do you think they are feeling as they wait?
  - What do they think their mother will bring back?
  - What do you think will happen next?

During reading

- Listen as children are reading and comment on good expression. Praise participation in discussion, particularly individuals who initiate comments and give relevant responses

REVISIT AND RESPOND

Bring the group back together and discuss some of the points below.

Note: Since there are only 20 minutes for each session, you are advised to focus on only one or two of the elements that are listed below.

- Talk about how the illustrations indicate whether it is day or night. Ask the children to find evidence of what time it is when the baby owls come out of their house. (Stars in the sky.)

- Turn to spread 6 and ask: *What word describes the wood at night? What words tell us that wild things might be lurking in the wood?* ('...things *moved* all around'.) *What sort of things could they be? Can you name some creatures that come out at night? What sort of noises do you think the owls might hear?* Ask children to try making some of these noises using their voices. (For example: hooting, rustling, crackling, squeaking and howling.) Ask the children to search the illustrations for creatures. Ask: *Why do you think they are all out of sight? Where might they be hiding?*

- Talk about how the illustrator uses a black pen to create the illusion of darkness and shadows. Notice how small the babies look on spread 6 as they sit in a tree in the middle of the wood. Discuss how the dark, spooky wood surrounding them helps the reader to understand how scared they are feeling.

- Explore the illustrations of the owls and discuss the position of their perches. Establish the meaning of 'perch'. Ask: *What can you see on the first illustration that shows how the baby owls grip their perches?* (Strong talons.) *Can you describe the size and position of Sarah's/Percy's branches? Why is Sarah on the biggest branch? What is Bill perching on? Do you think the other owls could sit on this perch? Who is on the lowest perch? Which perch is the strongest/weakest?*

- Recall the earlier owl conversation. Find the inverted commas on spreads 5 and 6 and re-read the two short conversations the owls have. Ask: *What does Sarah say to make her younger brothers feel better?* Discuss how Percy extends Sarah's comment about Owl Mother coming back by adding the word *'soon!'*. Ask: *Why is the word 'soon' written in italics with an exclamation mark after it?* (To emphasise it.) *What clues do Percy's words give us about how he is feeling?* (He is worried/scared.) *What do you notice about Bill's two sentences? How do they compare with his sentences on the earlier pages?* (He repeats them.) *What does this say about his feelings?* (He misses his mummy; he is scared.) Having explored the conversation fully, re-read it with individuals reading the words of the owls, trying to reflect the contrasting voices.

- Discuss the strong family bonds between the babies. Ask: *Which owl looks after the others? Which owl tries to be brave but still needs reassurance? Who is the owl baby needing most reassurance? How can older brothers and sisters help us when we are anxious or in trouble? How can we help younger family members or friends?*

- Recall how apostrophes show the place of missing letters. Ask: *How many apostrophes can you find in this section? Which two words are shortened to create 'didn't' and 'She'll'?*

Ask the children to revisit the text and illustrations to support their answers. Encourage them to read aloud to the group when quoting text, and to initiate and respond to comments.

ASSESSMENT OPPORTUNITIES

The following bank of question prompts provides a quick and easy means of monitoring the children's comprehension skills and understanding of the text. The children's answers to a question must be supported by evidence from the text.

Understanding

- In what order do the baby owls speak?

- If you could ask Sarah a question about being the oldest owl baby, what would you ask?

- What do you think Sarah means by 'things that are nice'? What would an owl think was nice?

Inferences

- Why do the baby owls always stay near one another?

- Why do they stay near their house?

- Why did the baby owls need to be brave in the wood at night? Have you ever had to be brave, and what did you do?

Predicting

- What would happen if the owls all chose to perch on the ivy?

- How could the owls be in danger? What could happen to them?

- What do you think will happen in the next section?

Main ideas

- What do the owls talk about in this section?

- Why do you think Owl Mother has left her babies alone?

- Why do you think there are exclamation marks after all of Percy's and Bill's sentences? Does this affect the way you read them?

Language, structure and presentation

- What do you notice about the words 'nice' and 'mice'? Can you think of any other words that rhyme with them?

- Which adjectives describe the perches the owls choose?

- Why are some words written in italics?

Themes and conventions

- Have you read any other stories set in a dark wood? What did you like about them?

- The number three occurs often in traditional stories. What occurs in three in this story?

SESSION 3: WISHES COME TRUE!

SESSION AIMS

Explain clearly their understanding of what is read to them.

READ

- Ask the children to read the next three spreads (7 to 9) independently. Invite them to consider some of these questions.
  - What happens in this section?
  - Why do you think Sarah suggests that her brothers move to sit on her branch to wait?
  - What did the owls think might have happened to Owl Mother?
  - What did the owls close their eyes and wish for?
  - Which three words have the most importance to the story so far? ('AND SHE CAME'.)

During reading

- Listen as the group are reading and praise individuals for clear diction. Comment positively on those who show a good understanding of what they have read.

REVISIT AND RESPOND

Bring the group back together and discuss some of the points below.

Note: Since there are only 20 minutes for each session, you are advised to focus on only one or two of the elements that are listed below.

- Re-read the first two lines on spread 7 together. Ask: *Where have you read similar lines to these before?* (On the third spread.) *Why do you think the author has repeated them here?* (To emphasise that owls think a lot.) *Do you think the owls will still be thinking about where there mother is? Will they be more worried as even more time goes by without Owl Mother returning?*

- Read the rest of spread 7 together. Ask: *Why is it best for all the owls to sit on Sarah's branch? Do you think this a good suggestion? Why do you think the author has used the words 'all three together'?*

(To emphasise that the owls feel safer when they are closer.) *Do you think Sarah's suggestion that Owl Mother might have got lost is a likely one?* (If children do not seem to understand this question, pose the notion that a grown-up owl would not get lost because she should know her way around her own woods.)

- Recall discussions about the owls' pattern of speech on the earlier spreads. Ask: *Does the same pattern occur in this section? Who speaks first? Who follows? Does this repetition help the story to flow? Does Bill say the same words?* Ask: *Have you ever heard a very young child trying to talk? What sort of words or sounds does he or she say? Do you think that Bill's few words show that he is a very young owl just learning to talk?*

- Explain the meaning of 'atmosphere' and talk about how the author and illustrator create a scary atmosphere that reflects the mood of the frightened owls. Draw attention to the way the artist uses black lines on a blue or green background to represent trees and vegetation in the wood. This creates a dark, shadowy appearance in contrast to the clearer image of the little white owls alone on their branch. Now focus on the images of the owls. Discuss how they are huddled together and what this conveys about how they are feeling. Draw attention to their big round eyes on spread 7. Ask: *Why do you think the owls are so alert with wide anxious eyes? Why have they closed their eyes on the next page? Do you close your eyes to make a wish? Looking at these illustrations, how well do you think the illustrator has managed to add atmosphere?*

- Turn to spread 9 and ask: *Why do you think there are just three words on this page? Why do you think they are in capital letters? Why do you think the artist decided on a very large image of Owl Mother returning? How important to the story do you think this event is?*

Ask the children to revisit the text and illustrations to support their answers. Encourage them to read aloud to the group when quoting text.

ASSESSMENT OPPORTUNITIES

The following bank of question prompts provides a quick and easy means of monitoring the children's comprehension skills and understanding of the text. The children's answers to a question must be supported by evidence from the text.

Understanding

- What are the owls still thinking about?
- If you could ask Sarah why she thinks Owl Mother might have got lost, what do you think she would say?

Inferences

- When Sarah asks her brothers to sit on her branch, they move straight away. Why do you think they are keen to do this? Why do you think the owls are happier sitting together rather than on separate perches?
- Explain clearly what you understand by what Percy means when he says a fox might have 'got' Owl Mother.

Predicting

- Did you predict that Owl Mother would return in this section?
- What did you think Owl Mother would bring with her?

Main ideas

- Why are the last three words written in capitals?
- Do you like the way the owl conversations have a regular pattern? Is it satisfying to know what is coming next when you read a story? Why do you think this?

Language, structure and presentation

- Why are Sarah's words 'all' and 'my' written in italics?
- Read the sentence about the baby owls making a wish. Which word is repeated three times? Do you think this repetition is effective?
- What do you notice about the punctuation at the end of Percy's and Bill's sentences? (Exclamation marks.) Does it affect the way you read their words?

Themes and conventions

- Repetition is a key feature in traditional stories. What is repeated in this section?
- Making a wish occurs often in traditional stories. What do the owls wish for in this story? Does their wish come true? When is it traditional to close your eyes and make a wish? (Blowing out birthday cake candles.)

▼ SESSION 4: WHAT'S ALL THE FUSS?

SESSION AIMS

Link what they read or listen to with their own experiences.

READ

- Ask the children to read the last three spreads independently, considering some of these questions.
  - What happens in this part of the story?
  - How do the baby owls react to Owl Mother's arrival?
  - What does Owl Mother say to her excited babies?
  - Where does the story end? How do you know this?
  - Do you think this is a good ending? Why do you think this?

During reading

- As you listen to the group reading, praise individuals for good variation in expression.

REVISIT AND RESPOND

Bring the group back together and discuss some of the points below.

Note: Since there are only 20 minutes for each session, you are advised to focus on only one or two of the elements that are listed below.

- Recall the large image of Owl Mother returning on spread 9 and explore the illustration on spread 10. Ask children to find the baby owls on their branch and Owl Mother as she flies in. Explain the word 'vulnerable' as being in a place where you could be easily hurt or attacked, and say that you think the babies look vulnerable in this picture. Read the words accompanying this illustration together. Ask: *Which words tell us about the movement of Owl Mother and the sound she made? Can you show a swooping movement using your hand, and hold out your arms in the same way Owl Mother holds her wings as she flies? How has the artist made the owl babies look vulnerable in this picture?* (They are tiny and in the open.)

- Read spread 11 and discuss the verbs used to describe the movement of the babies when Owl Mother lands. ('flapped', 'danced' and 'bounced') Ask the group how we know that this happened in the past. (The 'ed' ending.) Ask: *What do the words tell us about how the babies are feeling?* Concentrate on the word 'Mummy!' and ask: *Why do you think this is the first time the babies have all spoken together? How do you think they would say this word? What clues help you?* (The word 'cried', movement verbs, exclamation mark, illustration.) *What other punctuation could the author have used to emphasise their excitement?* (Italics, capitals.) *What effect do you think using the word 'and' four times in this sentence has?* (Emphasises the excited movements of the babies, especially if read quickly!) Encourage children to relate the owl babies' reaction to their own reactions to exciting experiences.

- Re-read the last page together and ask: *When Owl Mother gets her babies back into their house, what does she say to them? Why do you think she uses the words 'WHAT'S ALL THE FUSS?' Why are her words written in capitals? What makes Owl Mother confident that her babies would know she was coming back? Why did the owls have to think about their mother's statement? Do you think they had doubts about her return? What do you think this book tells us about the importance of family?*

- Recall the repeated words of Bill in every section so far. Ask: *Why does Bill say something different here? How do you think he is feeling now? Bill has the last word in the story. Do you think this is a good way to end it?*

- Compare the illustrations of the owl family in their house on the first and last spreads of the book. Ask: *What is different about the babies in the two pictures? Why are they fussing around their mother at the end of the story? What is Owl Mother doing on both pictures?* (Looking lovingly at her babies.) *Do you think the babies are safe and secure in their own house? Where do you feel most secure?*

- Depending on the edition, explore the front and back inner covers and discuss the pattern and colours the illustrator has used. Ask: *What do you notice about the design on these pages?* (Resembles light through trees/feathers.) *Why has the artist used browns?* (Colours of Owl Mother's feathers/trees.) *Do you like this design? Do you think it reflects the theme of the book?*

Ask the children to revisit the text and illustrations to support their answers. Encourage them to link with their own experiences when relevant – for example, being alone or excited.

ASSESSMENT OPPORTUNITIES

The following bank of question prompts provides a quick and easy means of monitoring the children's comprehension skills and understanding of the text. The children's answers to a question must be supported by evidence from the text.

Understanding
- What question would you like to ask Owl Mother?
- Have you ever felt worried or excited like the owl babies? Can you describe these feelings?

Inferences
- Why do owls fly softly and silently? How will this help when they are hunting?
- Do you think the baby owls can fly yet? What evidence is there for your answer?

Predicting
- Do you think Owl Mother will tell her babies before she goes out again? Why do you think this?
- If there was a sequel to this story, what would you like to happen?

Main ideas
- What would you like to ask the author or illustrator about this book?
- What part do the illustrations play in this section, and in the book altogether?
- Do you think this book carries a message? (Family love.)

Language, structure and presentation
- The story starts and ends in the same setting and moves out of it in the middle. Why do you think this is a good structure for a story?
- Which statement does the author repeat for the third time in this section? Why did the owls have to think a lot about what their mother said to them?

Themes and conventions
- What did you like best about this final part?
- What words could the author add to the end so that it has a traditional ending?

SESSION 1: THE HUNT BEGINS!

SESSION AIMS

Discuss the significance of the title and events; predict what might happen.

READ

- Ask the children to explore the cover and read the first four spreads independently. Invite them to consider some of these questions.
  - What do you think the title tells us about what the story is about?
  - How has the author separated each event in the story?
  - What is meant by the word 'hunt'? Have you ever hunted for something you have lost?
  - Which two outdoor features do the characters pass through?
  - What do you think will happen next?

During reading

- Listen while the group are reading, praising any individuals who recognise and express the rhythmic repetition of the words. Comment positively on attempts to predict future events based on evidence read.

REVISIT AND RESPOND

Bring the group back together and discuss some of the points below.

Note: Since there are only 20 minutes for each session, you are advised to focus on only one or two of the elements that are listed below.

- Explore the cover illustration together. Ask: *Do you think the people belong to the same family or are good friends? Do you think the tallest character is the children's father, brother or friend? Why do you think the little girl is walking on tiptoes/the boy carrying a stick? Why is the smallest child being carried? What is the dog sniffing at on the back cover? What do you think might happen to these people in the story?*

- Read the first paragraph on the back cover together. Ask: *Who do you think is going on a bear hunt? Can you describe the bear they hope to catch? Why do they say they are not scared? Do you think they are telling the truth? How would you feel if you were hunting a bear? How do you know that the weather is suitable for going hunting?*

- Read the first spread and explore the accompanying illustration together. Ask: *Where have you read the first four lines before?* (On the back cover.) *Who do you think is telling the story? Do you think it is one member of the group or all of them? Why do you need to think about this?* (Repetition of 'We'/'We're'.)

- Ask the children about the first obstacle that the characters have to get through. Can they find two adjectives used by the storytellers to describe this grass? ('Long wavy'.) Talk about what the characters are doing in the illustration on the first spread as they tackle the grass. (Arms in the air, jumping, helping each other, pushing.) Encourage the children to predict the sound that long wavy grass might make as they push through it. Read the next spread and ask: *Do you think these words describe this sound well? Did you predict a similar sound? What do you notice about the two words?* (Only one letter is different.) *Why do you think the sound is repeated three times?* (To emphasise the rhythm.)

- Read spreads 3 and 4 and discuss the next obstacle (a 'deep cold river'), asking similar questions about the pattern of word repetition, adjectives and 'sound' words. Point out the importance of the illustrations in providing extra information.

- Investigate the role of exclamation marks in the first four spreads. Identify them together and ask children how they should read the word preceding each one. Ask: *Why do you think there is an exclamation mark after the second word of each repeated sound? Does it make a difference if you say the second word more loudly, higher or lower? What is this difference?* (Emphasises rhythm and pattern.)

- Explain that a hyphen is used to connect two words, or parts of words. Then draw attention to the hyphen used to connect the two sounds in 'Uh-uh!'

- Talk about how the repeated lines create a poetic rhythm. Predict whether this will continue into the next section.

Ask the children to revisit the text and illustrations to support their answers. Encourage them to read quotes aloud to the group, and praise predictions backed up by good evidence.

ASSESSMENT OPPORTUNITIES

The following bank of question prompts provides a quick and easy means of monitoring the children's comprehension skills and understanding of the text. The children's answers to a question must be supported by evidence from the text.

Understanding

- Can you describe the characters introduced in this section?
- How do the characters support one another?
- If you could ask one of the characters a question about this part of the story, who would it be and what would you ask?

Inferences

- Why do the characters say they cannot go over or under the grass? Which creatures could do this?
- What structures or objects do people build to help them to go over or under rivers?
- How did the characters keep their shoes dry when they crossed the river?
- Why is it easy for the dog to cross the river? How does the dog help the boy?

Predicting

- Do you think the characters put themselves in danger by wading through the deep cold river? Why do you think this?
- Which character will stay the driest during the river crossing?
- What do you think will happen in the next section?

Main ideas

- Why would a bear hunt be a scary experience?
- How does the text on the first page set the scene for the story?
- How does the setting change in this section?

Language, structure and presentation

- Do you think this section is like a poem, even though there is no regular rhyming pattern? Why do you think this? Do you think this effect will continue throughout the book?
- Which adjectives describe the grass and river?

Themes and conventions

- Do you think this story is about real or fantasy events? Explain why you think this.
- Who do you think is telling this story?

SESSION 2: MESSY AND SCARY

SESSION AIMS

Link what they read or listen to with their own experiences.

READ

- Ask the children to read spreads 5 to 8 independently, considering some of the following questions.
  - In what way does this section sound like the previous one? Which lines are repeated?
  - What is the most dangerous obstacle for the characters to go through? Why do you think this?
  - Have you ever walked through a big dark forest? Can you describe this experience?

During reading

- While the group are reading, praise children who recognise and comment on the continuing rhythm of the words from the previous section. Comment positively on any attempts to link events to their own experiences.

REVISIT AND RESPOND

Bring the group back together and discuss some of the points below.

Note: Since there are only 20 minutes for each session, you are advised to focus on only one or two of the elements that are listed below.

- Read spreads 5 to 8 together and make links with the first four spreads. Ask: *Which lines are almost the same? Which words are different?* (Those describing new obstacles and their associated sounds or movements.) *Do you like the fact that the text follows a pattern? Does it help you to predict what might happen next?*

- Discuss the children's experiences of 'thick oozy mud'. Ask them if they have ever walked through mud and to describe what this felt like. What sound did it make? Do they think the words 'Squelch squerch!' describe this sound well? Encourage them

to try exchanging the letter that is different in each word with another to create a new sound that is equally effective. (For example: squench, squeuch, squeech, squewch.) Ask: *Can you describe what the author means by 'oozy' mud? Have you ever felt mud oozing between your fingers or toes, or watched it oozing around your boots? How does the illustration of the characters trying to squelch through the mud show that it is 'thick' and 'oozy'? Do they seem to be having difficulty balancing?*

- Read the adjectives describing the characters negotiating the forest. ('Stumble trip!') Ask: *What do you think these words describe? Is it sound or movement? Who do you think is stumbling and tripping?* Talk about what sort of things the characters might stumble and trip over in a forest.

- Focus on the rhythm of the language on spread 8 by asking children to clap the words as you read the page, emphasising the word 'trip' with a louder clap. Ask: *Do you think this demonstrates the rhythm of the hunt through the forest? How else could the author have emphasised the word 'trip' to create this rhythm?* (Capital, larger or bold letters, or italics.)

- Explore the illustrations relating to the 'big dark forest'. Ask: *How do you think the characters feel as they sit and dry their muddy feet and look at the forest looming ahead? What do their expressions tell us? How do you think the little boy is feeling as he runs towards it waving his stick? Do you think the girl is eager to get going as she points to the forest? What do you think she is saying? Why do you think the baby does not look scared? What happens when they enter the forest? Who is leading the way now? If you were one of the characters at this point, which one would you be and would you want to go through the big dark forest?*

- Look at the illustrations of the characters preparing to go through the mud and the forest (spreads 5 and 7). Recall earlier discussion about whether the characters are a family or good friends. Make links to the children's own families and friends to support them in deciding. Ask: *Do you usually play with friends of your own age or lots of different ages? Do you often have a baby playing with you when you are with your friends? Do your answers make you think this is more likely to be a family? Who do you think the tallest character is? How are they helping one another? How do your family support one another?*

Ask the children to revisit the text and illustrations to support their answers. Encourage them to read aloud to the group, and praise them for making direct links to their own experiences.

ASSESSMENT OPPORTUNITIES

The following bank of question prompts provides a quick and easy means of monitoring the children's comprehension skills and understanding of the text. The children's answers to a question must be supported by evidence from the text.

Understanding

- Which is the messiest obstacle in this section? What evidence is there of how messy the characters became?
- Why did the characters take off their shoes before crossing the mud?
- Why is the boy waving his stick as he runs to the forest?

Inferences

- Do you think any of the characters might want to turn back at the sight of the forest? Which one(s)?

Predicting

- What do you think will happen to the characters in the forest?
- Do you think they will meet the bear? Why do you think this?

Main ideas

- What do you think is the most frightening obstacle the characters have to go through in this section?
- What do you think the dog enjoys most – the mud

or the forest? Why do you say this? Why is the dog sniffing the air before going into the forest?

Language, structure and presentation

- What have you noticed about the pattern of the text? What do you like about it? Is there anything you think should be changed?
- Do you think the forest is scary? Which adjectives give clues about this? Can you think of adjectives to describe a forest that is not scary?

Themes and conventions

- Which obstacle in this section can usually be found in a fantasy or fairy story? (The forest.)

SESSION 3: GETTING NEARER!

SESSION AIMS

Recognise and join in with predictable phrases.

READ

- Ask the children to read spreads 9 to 12 independently. Invite them to consider some of these questions.

  - How does the weather change in this section?
  - What do you think it would be like to be out in a snowstorm?
  - What do you think the characters feel about going into the cave?
  - What do you think will happen in the next section?

During reading

- While the group are reading, comment positively on individuals who use good expression that reflects the content. Praise those who recognise and begin to chant the predictable rhythm of the words.

REVISIT AND RESPOND

Bring the group back together and discuss some of the points below.

Note: Since there are only 20 minutes for each session, you are advised to focus on only one or two of the elements that are listed below.

- Read spreads 9 to 12 together and invite the children to join in with the chant on the first and third pages. Ask individuals to read a line each and try to keep the same rhythm going. Suggest that the person reading the line 'We're not scared' whispers this for added effect. Ask: *Do you think the characters chant these words as they continue their hunt? Do you think chanting like this will help them when they are frightened or tired?*

- Look closely at the words of the chant and draw attention to the contractions. Recall the use of an apostrophe to replace letters that have been removed. Ask: *Which word has an apostrophe?* ('We're') *Which letter has been removed from the word 'are'? What is the effect on the rhythm if you read the words without contracting them?* Read the rest of the spread and identify the contractions 'can't' and 'We've'. Question the children about them in the same way.

- Read the description of the snowstorm together and discuss the accompanying illustrations. Ask: *Have you ever been out in a snowstorm? What did it feel like? Which words describe the way the snowflakes are moving? Have you ever noticed snowflakes moving like this? What do you think makes them swirl and whirl? How can you tell by the illustrations that there is a storm coming and that the wind is strong?* (Big black cloud, characters bent over, hair and clothes blowing.)

- After discussing the storm, ask: *What sound did the snowstorm make? Have you ever heard wind making this noise? Which letter is repeated to create this sound? Can you blow through cupped hands to make this sound?* (Show children how to do this if necessary.)

- Read the cave description together and explore the related illustrations. Ask: *Which two adjectives describe the cave? What is meant by 'gloomy'? How do you think the characters feel as they look into the entrance of the cave? What is the baby trying to do? How does the appearance of the dog show that it is reluctant to enter the cave?* (Drooping ears and tail, unhappy expression.) Ask the children if they would want to go into the cave themselves. Do they think the characters are scared? Talk about how the dark 'gloomy' shadows may add to the fear. Ask children to think about the sounds they might hear inside the cave and to share their ideas with a partner. (For example: loud or quiet; clear or muffled; would there be echoes?)

- Read the words accompanying the illustration of the inside of the cave together. Ask: *Why do you think the characters are on tiptoe? Why has the author repeated this word three times and added an exclamation mark each time? Do you think the characters have seen or heard something, or both, and so they are trying not to make a sound?*

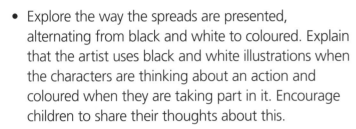

- Explore the way the spreads are presented, alternating from black and white to coloured. Explain that the artist uses black and white illustrations when the characters are thinking about an action and coloured when they are taking part in it. Encourage children to share their thoughts about this.

Ask the children to revisit the text and illustrations to support their answers. Encourage them to read aloud when quoting evidence to the group, and praise them for joining in expressively with repeated words and phrases.

ASSESSMENT OPPORTUNITIES

The following bank of question prompts provides a quick and easy means of monitoring the children's comprehension skills and understanding of the text. The children's answers to a question must be supported by evidence from the text.

Understanding

- Do you think the characters are dressed for a snowstorm?
- What clues can you see outside of the cave that show where it is situated? (Sea with a boat sailing.) What has happened to the weather? (Sunny again.)

Inferences

- Do you think the characters are brave by entering the cave? Why do you think this?
- Do you think a cave is a likely place to find a bear? Why?

Predicting

- Do you think it would be easy for the characters to get lost in the snowstorm? What makes you think this? Which character could guide them?
- Do you think a bear will appear?

Main ideas

- Why do you think the snowstorm is an unexpected event? (It was a beautiful day when they set out.)
- What sort of things would you expect to find in a cave?

Language, structure and presentation

- Which letters has the author added to the verbs 'whirl' and 'swirl' to make them into adjectives to describe the snowstorm?
- Why are the words 'WHAT'S THAT?' in bold capitals?

Themes and conventions

- Do you like the way this book is presented, with black and white then colour pages, or do you prefer one or the other? Which do you think is best, and why?
- What is your favourite character in this section, and why do you say this?

SESSION 4: IT'S A BEAR!!!

SESSION AIMS

Make inferences on the basis of what is said and done.

READ

- Ask the children to read the final four spreads independently, thinking about some of the following questions.
  - Did you predict correctly that a bear would be in the cave?
  - What do you know about the appearance of the bear from the text and illustrations?
  - How can you tell from the ending of the story that the characters are a family and not just a group of friends?
  - Was the ending as you expected? Did you like the way the story finishes? Why do you say this?

During reading

- While the group are reading, comment positively on individuals who use good expression and read with clarity. Praise those who quote relevant evidence when explaining inferences they have made.

REVISIT AND RESPOND

Bring the group back together and discuss some of the points below.

Note: Since there are only 20 minutes for each session, you are advised to focus on only one or two of the elements that are listed below.

- Re-read the final four spreads together, clapping whenever there is an exclamation mark to emphasise how many there are. Discuss how this punctuation mark helps us to understand how the author intends us to read the text. Ask: *Why do you think the author uses so many exclamation marks in this section? Do you think it is the most exciting section? Why? How do they affect the way you read the text?*

- Discuss the sentence structure in this section, drawing attention to the way the words are grouped in short phrases rather than longer sentences. Talk about the journey back home with the bear in pursuit. Ask: *Do you think the characters would complete their journey back in less time than it took them to get to the cave? Why do you think this? Why do you think the author has grouped words in short phrases to describe the journey home, and why does each of these phrases end in an exclamation mark? Do you find that you are reading it more quickly? Do you think this helps you to understand the fear and panic the characters are feeling? Do you think this is what the author wants you to do?*

- Explore the appearance of the spread showing the journey home. Ask the children to consider whether they have seen stories presented in strips like this anywhere else. (Perhaps in comic books.) Point out that the design encourages us to read the text in short sharp bursts, and ask the children why they think the artist has designed the page like this.

- Discuss the way the story ends, with the family shivering with fear in bed and the bear slowly ambling back to his cave. Ask: *Where do the family go as soon as they get into the house? Why do you think they forget to shut the door? Why is it important that the door is shut? Why do they go straight under the bed covers? What can you tell about their feelings from their expressions? Which character is the only one to look happy? Why do you think the characters say they will not go on a bear hunt again? How do you think the bear is feeling as the door is shut and as he looks through the window? What can you tell from the illustration of the bear as he wanders along the shore back to his cave? Is he angry, happy or sad? Why would he be sad?*

- After talking about the story ending, ask: *How do you feel about the way this story ends? Would you change anything?*

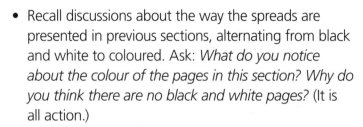

- Recall discussions about the way the spreads are presented in previous sections, alternating from black and white to coloured. Ask: *What do you notice about the colour of the pages in this section? Why do you think there are no black and white pages?* (It is all action.)

Ask the children to quote from the text and refer to illustrations to support their answers. Encourage them to read aloud when quoting evidence to the group, and praise individuals for using contextual clues discussed to influence their expression.

ASSESSMENT OPPORTUNITIES

The following bank of question prompts provides a quick and easy means of monitoring the children's comprehension skills and understanding of the text. The children's answers to a question must be supported by evidence from the text.

Understanding

- What do you think the dog and the bear think of one another? Use adjectives to describe their expressions.
- If you could ask the bear a question at the end of this story, what would it be?

Inferences

- Why do you think the bear chases after the characters? Do you think he is a dangerous bear?
- If you met this bear unexpectedly, what would you do?

Predicting

- What do you think will happen if the characters do not close the door in time?
- What do you think the bear will do now?

Main ideas

- Why do you think the characters turn and run when they see the bear?
- Did the characters follow the same route back home? How do you know this?

Language, structure and presentation

- Why are the words 'IT'S A BEAR!!!!' printed in bold capitals with four exclamation marks after them? How do you think you should read this?
- Why are the letters of the last sentence larger than those in the rest of the book? How else could the author have emphasised the importance of this sentence?

Themes and conventions

- Why is the journey home presented as a comic strip? What do you like/not like about books and magazines presented in this way?
- How does the last line of the story compare with the first line? Which two words have been added? ('not' and 'again') Why do the characters feel differently at the start and finish?

▼ SESSION 1: THE DRAGON SCHOOL

SESSION AIMS

Link what they read or listen to with their own experiences.

READ

- Ask the children to read the first four spreads independently. Invite them to consider some of these questions.
  - What do you know about the school in the story?
  - Who runs it and who are the pupils?
  - Who is the biggest dragon in the school?
  - What does this dragon try his hardest to win?

During reading

- Listen in to individual readers while the group reads. Praise clear diction and good expression. Comment on those who automatically make links with their own experiences as they discuss what they have read.

REVISIT AND RESPOND

Bring the group back together and discuss some of the points below.

Note: Since there are only 20 minutes for each session, you are advised to focus on only one or two of the elements that are listed below.

- Explore the front and back cover illustration and read them together. Ask: *What do you think the title tells us about the story and main character? Which dragon do you think is Zog? Which two objects does Zog have that might give a clue about the story?* (Golden star and plaster.) *Which dragon do you think might be the teacher? What is this dragon holding?* (A piece of chalk.) *What has the teacher drawn on the board?* (A princess.) *Who is the author of this book? Who is the illustrator? What do you expect this book will be like from the clues on the cover and what you know of the author and illustrator?* (For example: funny, rhyming, fantasy, magic.)

- Discuss the illustration on the inner page. Ask: *Who do you think these dragons are? Do you recognise one of them? Where do you think he is going? Given the information you already have, do you think this could be Zog on his way to school? Where does Zog live? Does he have brothers or sisters? Are they younger or older?*

- Explore the first spread, discussing the illustration and then reading the text together. Ask: *Can you identify Zog? How can you tell by what he is doing that he is the keenest dragon?* (Hand up and hopping up and down eagerly.) *What is Madam Dragon holding? What do you know about the importance of the golden stars to Zog?*

- Focus on the dragon school and make comparisons with the children's own experience of school. Ask: *Where is the dragon school set? Are there any buildings? What are your school buildings like? What sort of lessons do you have outdoors? What has Madam Dragon been teaching the dragons about?* (Point out the drawings on the board.) *What does your teacher use instead of a blackboard and chalk? What does Madam Dragon give dragons as a reward for achievement? What sort of rewards are you given?*

- Discuss the meaning of unfamiliar words, such as 'fearsome', 'implore', 'champion' and 'keenest'. Ask questions to ensure the children understand them in context; for example: *Can you think of a way to describe the force of Zog's roar without using the word 'fearsome'?*

- Discuss the phrases 'many moons ago' and 'through the blue'. Ask: *Do you think Madam Dragon ran her school recently or a long time ago? Why do you think this? How often does the moon appear? How long is 'many moons'? What common story language could the author have used?* (A long time ago.) *Which version sounds better? Where was Zog flying when he 'zigzagged through the blue'? What colour was the sky? Why do you think the author has left out the word 'sky'?* Invite the children to try reading the two lines with 'sky' added, and talk about what effect this has on the rhyme.

Discuss the use of exclamation marks, and why the author uses them frequently when characters are speaking. Re-read the words preceding them, placing added emphasis on them. Decide together whether this gives greater meaning to the content. Draw attention to the ellipsis after the words 'loop…' and 'end…' when describing Zog's flying and roaring efforts. Pause after each one to create dramatic effect before reading what happens next. Ask: *Why do you think it is a good idea to pause for effect after these words? What happens to Zog afterwards?*

Briefly recall the use of suffixes in reference to the words 'keenest', 'biggest' and 'hardest', and discuss how the meaning changes with the addition of the suffix.

Ask the children to search the text for appropriate evidence for their answers. Encourage them to read their evidence aloud. Praise individuals who make links with their own experiences.

ASSESSMENT OPPORTUNITIES

The following bank of question prompts provides a quick and easy means of monitoring the children's comprehension skills and understanding of the text. The children's answers to a question must be supported by evidence from the text.

Understanding
- Where do you think the little girl came from and what useful things did she have in her bag?
- What do the dragons learn in Year One and Year Two?

Inferences
- What are the differences between the dragon school and your own school?
- What are the differences between Madam Dragon and your own teacher?
- What does your teacher use instead of a blackboard and chalk?

Predicting
- Do you think Zog will ever win a golden star?

Main ideas
- Can you describe the setting from clues in the illustrations?
- Why, and how, does the little girl help Zog?

Language, structure and presentation
- How does the author change the words 'big', 'keen' and 'hard' so that we know that Zog is bigger, keener and tries harder than any of the other dragons?
- Which word does Madam Dragon use when she pleads with the dragons to roar louder?

Themes and conventions
- What do you like about the way this story is written?
- What do dragons usually do in stories? Why do young dragons need to learn to fly and roar?

Recognise and join in with predictable phrases.

READ

- Ask the children to read spreads 5 to 8 independently, bearing in mind some of these questions.
  - What do the dragons learn in Year Three and Year Four?
  - How does the little girl help Zog in this section?
  - What did Madam Dragon ask the dragons to breathe from their mouths?
  - What came out of the dragons' mouths at first?
  - What happened to Zog when he finally managed to breathe fire?

During reading

- Listen to individual readers while the rest of the group read. Comment positively if individuals use contrasting voices to represent the dragon and little girl. Praise those who begin to notice repetition of text from the first section.

REVISIT AND RESPOND

Bring the group back together and discuss some of the points below.

Note: Since there are only 20 minutes for each session, you are advised to focus on only one or two of the elements that are listed below.

- As you re-read spreads 5 to 8 together, discuss the meaning of words children are not sure of, such as 'soothing', 'fumes' and 'triumph'. Ask questions to check their understanding; for example: *Have you ever sucked a peppermint to sooth a sore throat? Did it make you feel better? Can you think of another word for 'soothing'?* Discuss the phrase 'all his might', referring to the need to use all of your strength to achieve something. Talk about how Zog used all of his strength and energy to try to blow fire.

- Explore Madam Dragon's words and notice that she repeats the same two lines after she instructs the dragons, only substituting the words describing what the dragons are learning ('breathing bonfires' in this section). Encourage the children to repeat the two lines individually around the group, in their best 'dragon teacher' voices, before saying them together in unison. Now read the last two lines in this section. Ask: *What do you notice about the slight change in these words?* ('You'll need to capture hundreds'.) *Do you like the way Madam Dragon repeats her words? Do you think she encourages the dragons with these words? Do you think she is a good teacher?*

- Identify the repetition each time the little girl arrives. Read the relevant lines one after the other to emphasise the similarity, and point out any differences. Repeat them several times together. Do the same with the two lines of Zog's words that start 'What a good idea!' Recall him using these words in the same context in the first section. Discuss why authors use such repetition and whether it is satisfying for the reader to be able to predict word patterns.

- Revise the use of regular punctuation, such as inverted commas, exclamation and question marks, asking children for examples from the text as evidence. Recall the use of contractions to shorten words and find examples within the text. Ask: *Which word has been shortened by the apostrophe in the contractions 'you'd'/'you've'/'you'll'/ 'you're'? Which letters have been removed in each one?* Draw attention to the ellipsis and recall its use from discussions on the earlier spreads. Find the ellipsis on the page depicting Zog practising fire breathing. Compare this with the earlier page where Zog was practising roaring. Draw attention to the fact that it occurs immediately before something goes wrong in each case. Ask: *Do you think that pausing increases the dramatic effect?*

- Explore the artwork depicting Zog practising breathing fire and discuss how this is presented as individual images compared with the full illustration on other pages. Recall that this design was also used in the first section when Zog practised flying and roaring. Discuss the benefits of presenting several images on one page, rather like a comic strip.

- Talk about the importance of illustration in introducing extra information and explore images to find tiny detail. Ask: *How many different kinds of bird can you spot? How many wild animals can you name? What features tell us about the landscape?* (For example: distant mountains, forests, rocks, trees, paths, pond and grass.)

Ask the children to try to discover evidence for their answers within the text and then to read this evidence aloud. Praise individuals who show clear recognition of when there is repetition in the text.

ASSESSMENT OPPORTUNITIES

The following bank of question prompts provides a quick and easy means of monitoring the children's comprehension skills and understanding of the text. The children's answers to a question must be supported by evidence from the text.

Understanding
- Why did the girl offer Zog a bandage?
- Why did the dragons make scarecrow princesses?

Inferences
- What did Madam Dragon mean when she said the dragons would be breathing bonfires?
- Why did Zog twirl around in triumph? What was he celebrating?

Predicting
- Do you think Zog will manage to capture a princess?
- Will Zog have another accident that needs help?
- What sort of things do you think will happen in the next section?

Main ideas
- What effect did the twirling have on the fire Zog was breathing?
- Why did Zog lie in the pond?

Language, structure and presentation
- Which of Madam Dragon's words are easy to remember? Why do you think the author includes so much repetition?
- Which of Zog's words does he like to repeat? What do you think of this use of repetition?
- Why has the author indicated a pause as Zog twirls around in triumph? What comes next?

Themes and conventions
- What clues help you to recognise that this might be a fairy story? (Castle, ruins in background, dragons breathing fire, capturing princesses.)
- What do you notice about the way the artist presents images of Zog learning to breathe fire? How does this compare with the illustration on the other pages? Which style do you prefer?

▼ SESSION 3: THE GOLDEN STAR AT LAST!

SESSION AIMS

Become very familiar with fairy stories, retelling them and considering their characteristics.

READ

- Ask the children to read spreads 9 to 12 independently. Invite them to consider some of these questions.
  - What is the little girl's real name?
  - How does she help Zog?
  - What does Zog do to achieve his ambition?
  - What do the dragons learn in Year Five?
  - Why did the knight ride into the dragon school?

During reading

- Listen in to individuals as the group reads. Praise clear, expressive reading. Comment positively on those who demonstrate an awareness of the fairytale genre during discussions.

REVISIT AND RESPOND

Bring the group back together and discuss some of the points below.

Note: Since there are only 20 minutes for each session, you are advised to focus on only one or two of the elements that are listed below.

- Recall previous discussions about the importance of illustration and how it provides additional information. Focus on the tower illustration. Ask children why this suggests that this is a fairy tale. (A tower, princess in window, dragon, typical old lady, story book bear, people fighting from turreted walls.) Explore the illustration of the knight on spread 11 and typical features such as a horse, armour, spurs, helmet and sword. Notice how the illustrations indicate that the dragons improvised when practising fighting by riding on each other's backs with wooden swords and shields.

- Discuss the meaning of words children are not sure of, such as 'congratulations', 'trusty' and 'agog'. Explain that something that is 'trusty' can always be relied upon. Ask: *Why does Sir Gadabout describes his sword as 'trusty'?* Explain that being 'agog' over something is feeling really excited and eager to know more about it. Ask: *What does it feel like to be 'agog' over something? What makes you 'agog'?*

- Re-read the text together, asking children to listen for repetition from previous sections. Notice how the princess continues to use the word 'Perhaps…' before making a suggestion, and Zog still uses the comment 'What a good idea!' in response. They still 'zigzag through the blue' and the author still starts the sentence about learning with 'A year went by'. Ask: *Do you enjoy the way Zog and the princess repeat familiar phrases, and that the text is predictable in parts? How does it help you to remember and retell the story?*

- Draw attention to the use of italics for the word *'never'* on spread 9 when Zog comments on winning a golden star. Discuss why the author uses this feature to emphasise the word. Try re-reading the sentence with added emphasis. Ask: *Does writing the word in this way affect the way you read it? What else could the author have done to emphasise this word?* (Capitals, bold, larger font.)

- Explore the illustration of Zog's golden star presentation on spread 10 and invite individuals to retell the scene. Ask: *What do you think Madam Dragon is saying to Zog? What do you think Zog is saying? Why is he pointing to Princess Pearl? Do you think he is explaining about her part in his achievement? Which two adjectives describe how Zog felt when he won the golden star?* ('proud' and 'happy'.) *Why do you think Princess Pearl felt good as well? How did she help Zog to win the star? Have you ever felt proud and happy about an achievement? Can you describe your achievement, and how it felt to be proud? Have you ever helped someone to achieve something? What did you do and how did you feel?*

- Explore the last page in this section, depicting Sir Gadabout about to rescue the princess. Discuss the fairytale elements in both the text and illustration. Ask: *How many fairytale characters can you name? What is typical about the appearance of Sir Gadabout? How can you tell that the little girl is really a princess? What has the knight come to do?*

Invite the children to find evidence for their answers within the text, and read or retell this as evidence. Praise individuals who show understanding of the fairytale genre.

ASSESSMENT OPPORTUNITIES

The following bank of question prompts provides a quick and easy means of monitoring the children's comprehension skills and understanding of the text. The children's answers to a question must be supported by evidence from the text.

Understanding

- What is the name of the knight?
- Where did Zog take Princess Pearl after he captured her?
- What did Princess Pearl enjoy doing for the dragons?
- If you could ask Sir Gadabout a question, what would it be?

Inferences

- What do you think Zog was referring to when he said 'I'm no good at this'?
- Why was Madam Dragon pleased when a real knight arrived? What was she teaching the dragons at the time that the knight could help with?

Predicting

- Who do you think will win the fight, Sir Gadabout or Zog?
- What do you think will happen in the next section?

Main ideas

- What did Madam Dragon present Zog with, and why?
- What do you know about knights/princesses? What do they look like and where do they live?
- Do you think the characters of Sir Gadabout and Princess Pearl are typical? Why do you say this?

Language, structure and presentation

- How does the author make the reader aware of the passing of time? ('A year went by and…', different learning each year.)
- What do you like about the rhyming pattern?
- Which letters does the author add to the word 'tight' to make a longer word (adverb) that describes how Princess Pearl hung on to Zog as they flew through the air? What is the word?

Themes and conventions

- What did you enjoy about the way rhyme features in this section?
- Can you describe the typical fairytale images in this section? (Princess in tower, knight on horseback, bear, dragons, princess.)

SESSION AIMS

Explain clearly their understanding of what is read to them.

READ

- Ask the children to read the final three spreads independently. Invite them to consider some of these questions.
  - What do Princess Pearl and Sir Gadabout really want to be?
  - Who does Sir Gadabout ask to train him to be a doctor?
  - Who acts as the ambulance, and how?
  - What happens to the knight's horse?
  - What do you think of the story ending?

During reading

- Listen as the group reads and praise individuals for reading with clarity. Comment positively on those who demonstrate an understanding of what they have read during their discussions.

REVISIT AND RESPOND

Bring the group back together and discuss some of the points below.

Note: Since there are only 20 minutes for each session, you are advised to focus on only one or two of the elements that are listed below.

- Re-read the text on spread 13 together and talk about what is about to happen. Ask: *Why did the princess stop the dragon and knight from fighting? What did she say the world was too full of? Do you agree with this? What do you think about real fighting? Can you explain how you feel about play fighting? Why did the princess say she did not want to be rescued? What do you think she dislikes about being a princess? What does she really want to do?*

- Look closely at the details within the illustrations together. Ask: *How many items of Sir Gadabout's armour can you name? What does a stethoscope look like? Which well-known Julia Donaldson character's face can you see on the horse's coat? What colour is the dragon with feathery wings?*

- Clarify the meaning of unfamiliar vocabulary, such as 'chumps', 'stethoscope', 'Bravo!', 'career' and 'resounding', by putting the words into context. Break down the word 'resounding', explaining that the prefix 're' means to do something again. Discuss what a sound that is repeated over and over again is like, linking this to the word 'echo'. Have fun repeating the word 'Hurrah!' as a loud 'resounding' echo. Ask children to suggest words and phrases meaning 'Well done!', such as 'Congratulations!', 'Good job!', 'Excellent!' and 'Good for you!' Add 'Bravo!' to this list and pretend to be Madam Dragon cheering Zog for his achievement, with children choosing different words from the selection to shout out. Discuss what children would like to be when they grow up, using the word 'career' in this context.

- Invite children to find capital letters used for character names and the start of sentences. Ensure that they understand why capitals are used for the words 'Flying Doctor' and 'STOP'. Identify contractions used to shorten words. Ask: *Which two words have been shortened to create the following contractions: 'Don't', 'won't', 'world's'?* Spend time discussing the word 'won't', explaining that it represents the words 'will not'. Say that apostrophes can also be used to show that something belongs to someone, for example, 'people's', 'pupils''.

- Discuss the role of rhyme and 'joining words' (conjunctions) in maintaining the flow of the text. Draw children's attention to the use of 'And', 'But' and 'Then' to start lines. (Explain that it is permissible to use a capital if the text resembles a verse.)

- Discuss the final two lines of the text and how it was repeated in previous sections. Ask: *Do you think these lines make a good story ending? Why do you think this? What traditional language could the author have used instead?*

- Explore the illustration depicting the Flying Doctors leaving on the final spread. Discuss the content and the advantage of having two pages to spread this over. Ask: *How do you think the dragons feel as they wave goodbye to Zog and their new friends? How is the horse feeling as he sees the knight fly away? How do you feel when you wave goodbye to someone you care about? Why has the knight taken off his armour? Why is Zog carrying a bag? Who does it belong to and what is inside it? What is the knight wearing round his neck? Why is he taking this with him?*

Invite the children to search the text for clues to support their answers, and then read them aloud to the rest of the group. Praise individuals who show understanding of the story content.

ASSESSMENT OPPORTUNITIES

The following bank of question prompts provides a quick and easy means of monitoring the children's comprehension skills and understanding of the text. The children's answers to a question must be supported by evidence from the text.

Understanding
- What is the difference between real and play fighting?
- Is real fighting a good thing to do?
- If you could ask Princess Pearl a question at the end of the story, what would it be?

Inferences
- What sort of clothes did Princess Pearl say she did not like? What do you think she likes wearing?
- Why did the horse have to stay behind at the end of the story?

Predicting
- Where do you think the Flying Doctors will fly to?
- What sort of adventures do you think they will have?

Main ideas
- Why did the princess tell Sir Gadabout and Zog to 'STOP'?
- How do you think this story helps us to realise the importance of caring for one another? Which character is a good role model for this?

Language, structure and presentation
- What did Madam Dragon mean when she said that being in a Flying Doctor crew would be an 'excellent career'?
- What did Princess Pearl mean when she called Zog and Sir Gadabout 'silly chumps'?
- Do you think the text flows smoothly? How does the author make sure this happens? (Rhymes, joining words.) Can you name some of the joining words she uses?

Themes and conventions
- Has this story changed your opinion of fairytale dragons, princesses and knights? How?
- If you wrote a sequel to this story, what would you call it?

SESSION 1: A BASKET OF FRUIT

SESSION AIMS

Check that the text makes sense to them as they read and correct inaccurate reading; predict what might happen.

READ

- Ask the children to read the first two spreads independently, considering some of these questions.
  - Can you name all seven fruits in the second picture?
  - Do you think that Handa picked the fruits herself?
  - Does Handa live in a cold or a hot country? Why do you think that?
  - Why does Handa have a ring on her head?
  - What do you think might happen next?

During reading

- Move around the group and 'tune in' to hear individuals read aloud. Encourage and praise good expression. Emphasise the need to check that the text makes sense to them, particularly as they tackle unfamiliar or difficult words

REVISIT AND RESPOND

Bring the group back together and discuss some of the points below.

Note: Since there are only 20 minutes for each session, you are advised to focus on only one or two of the elements that are listed below.

- Together, look at the front and back covers. Talk about the illustration on the front cover and ask the children what clues it gives as to what the book is about. Draw attention to the ostrich in the background. Read the blurb on the back cover aloud and ask the children what the mention of animals might mean for the story.

- Look at the illustrations on the first spread and talk about what you can see. How is Handa's appearance different to the children's, in terms of her hair and the clothes she wears? What does that tell the children about where she might live?

- Talk about the setting and ask: *Does Handa's country look like a hot or a cold country?* (The colours suggest a hot country – it is sunny and the sky is blue.) Ask the children to consider how Handa's country is different to theirs, and to give examples. They might, for instance, talk about the trees, the colour of the landscape and the presence of animals next to the houses. Ask: *Would you like to live there?*

- Read the first two spreads again as a whole group. Can the children see and name all seven fruits? (You could also look at the labelled illustrations of fruits on the front inner pages of the book.)

- Discuss whether the children think that Handa picked the fruits herself. Ask: *Do you think she bought them?* Ask the children if they could pick those fruits in this country. Which ones might they have to go to the supermarket for?

- Point out the ring on Handa's head in the right-hand picture on the first spread. Ask the children: *Why might she have the ring on her head?* (To help balance and steady the fruit basket.) *How does she put the basket onto her head?* (You could ask the children to mime this.) *Do you think this is a good way to carry things? How would you carry something heavy?*

- Do the children think Akeyo will be surprised when Handa gives her the fruit? Would they be surprised? Ask: *Which fruit do you think Akeyo will like best? Which is your favourite fruit?*

- Focus on the large illustration on the right-hand side of the second spread. Ask the children what else they can see. If necessary, draw attention to the tip of a tail in the tree. Ask: *What do you think it is? What animal might it belong to? What do you think might happen next?*

- To link with a maths element, you could ask the children to list the fruit in order of size – smallest to largest – based on the illustrations on the inner pages at the front. They could also make a guess about which is the sweetest, the softest, and so on.

Ask the children, whenever appropriate, to revisit the text to support their answers. Encourage the children to read aloud back to the group when referring back to the text – praise clear, confident and expressive reading.

ASSESSMENT OPPORTUNITIES

The following bank of question prompts provides a quick and easy means of monitoring the children's comprehension skills and understanding of the text. The children's answers to a question must be supported by evidence from the text.

Understanding

- Where is Handa setting off to with the fruit?
- What is Handa wondering as she walks along?
- Why do you think Handa uses a basket on her head to carry things?

Inferences

- Do you think Handa is looking forward to seeing her friend? Why do you think that?
- Do you think Handa has been to Akeyo's village before? How do you know that?

Predicting

- What animal do you predict is in the tree? Why do you think that?
- What might that animal do?
- What do you think will happen on Handa's journey?

Main ideas

- Who does Handa think will be surprised by the basket of fruit?

Language, structure and presentation

- Why do you think the author has used bright colours in her illustrations?
- The fruits are described as 'delicious'. Do you know what that word means? Can you suggest other words that mean the same thing? (For example: tasty, delightful, lovely, yummy.)
- Why has the author only shown the tail of the monkey in the picture? What is she trying to suggest by this?

Themes and conventions

- If a gift is made (or picked) for you, is this as good as a gift that is bought from a shop? Have you ever made a present for a friend? If so, what was it?

SESSION 2: MONKEY BUSINESS

SESSION AIMS

Search for clues to explain what might have happened and what might happen next.

READ

- Ask the children to read spreads 3 to 6 independently. While doing this, they should consider the following questions.
  - Do you think Handa sees the monkey?
  - Do you think the monkey is stealing?
  - Look out for the clues at the top left-hand side of the pages to see what has happened to the fruit.

During reading

- Move around the group and 'tune in' to hear individuals read aloud. Encourage and praise confident attempts to tackle unfamiliar words.

REVISIT AND RESPOND

Bring the group back together and discuss some of the points below.

Note: Since there are only 20 minutes for each session, you are advised to focus on only one or two of the elements that are listed below.

- Read the text on spread 3 again as a group. Remind the children of their predictions about the tail on the previous spread. Did they guess it belonged to a monkey? What clues helped them?

- Do the children think Handa sees the monkey? (The expression on her face doesn't suggest that she does.) Ask: *Does Handa know what's happened to the banana? Would she be cross if she knew?*

- Discuss the monkey on spread 3. Do the children think the monkey is stealing? Ask: *Could he be hungry? Could he be picking some fruit for himself? Would it be different if it was a person taking the fruit from the basket?*

- Re-read spreads 4, 5 and 6 and discuss them. Look at how Handa is pictured in each spread – does her expression change? Do the children think she is aware that something is happening to the fruit by the time the elephant has taken the mango? (Her eyes and eyebrows are key here.) Ask: *If she is aware that something is happening, why doesn't she do anything to stop it? If she doesn't know, then how can this be so if the basket is getting lighter from the stolen fruit?* (There are no correct answers here – this is just an opportunity for the children to back up their own argument.)

- Talk about the clues at the top left-hand side of the spreads that show what has happened to the fruit taken from Handa's basket. Encourage children to point out the banana skin being discarded on spread 4, and the ostrich and zebra walking away on spreads 5 and 6.

- Point out how the pictures are laid out in this section, with a smaller picture and text on the left-hand page and a full picture on the right side. Ask the group: *Why did the author do this?* (The left-hand page sets the scene, and the right-hand page shows what happens as a result.) Ask: *Does this work well?*

Ask the children, whenever appropriate, to revisit the text to support their answers. Encourage them to read aloud back to the group when referring back to the text – praise clear, confident and expressive reading.

ASSESSMENT OPPORTUNITIES

The following bank of question prompts provides a quick and easy means of monitoring the children's comprehension skills and understanding of the text. The children's answers to a question must be supported by evidence from the text.

Understanding

- Who is watching Handa as she passes by on spread 3?
- Who else is attracted to Handa's fruit basket as she walks along?
- What are the two pieces of yellow fruit in the basket?
- Which of the fruit is 'sweet-smelling'?
- Name the pieces of fruit that are left in the basket as Handa passes the zebra.
- List the different insects you can find on these pages.

Inferences

- Is Handa wondering if the monkey will like the 'soft yellow banana'? Explain why you say that.
- Do you think Handa has seen the monkey? How do you know that?
- Is the banana in the basket ripe? Explain how you know.
- Do you think Handa is aware that something is happening as she walks along? Why do you think this?
- Do you think Handa finds the basket heavy? Will she be tired from carrying it or not?
- Why do the animals choose the fruit they do, rather than something else?

Predicting

- Do you think Handa will be angry when she arrives at Akeyo's village and sees that the fruit is gone?
- What do you predict will happen by the time Handa reaches Akeyo's village? What clues suggest this to you?

Main ideas

- What does the monkey choose from the basket?
- Every time Handa wonders if her friend would like a particular fruit, it is taken and eaten. How does this make you feel?

Language, structure and presentation

- Why do you think the author has left a clue from the previous page on the top left-hand corner of each page?
- The guava is 'sweet-smelling'. How else might you describe this fruit from the information in the picture? (For example: small, yellow, shiny.)
- The author describes the orange as 'round' and 'juicy'. How would you describe the pineapple?
- What letters or sounds are repeated in the following: 'sweet-smelling' (/s/ sound) and 'ripe red' (/r/ sound)? What effect does this have on the way the language sounds? (You could mention alliteration here if desired.)

Themes and conventions

- Can animals 'steal' things? Or is it not possible because they don't know any better?
- Do you think Handa is safe walking through the African countryside on her own? Explain why you say that.

SESSION AIMS

Discuss word meanings, linking new meanings to those already known.

READ

- Ask the children to read spreads 7 to 10 independently. Ask them to consider some of these questions.
  - What is left in the basket when the parrot has stolen the passion fruit?
  - Why might Handa be suspicious about what is happening?
  - Look at the adjectives used to describe the fruit.
  - What might happen next? Look carefully at the pictures and background for clues.

During reading

- Move around the group and listen to each child read aloud. Encourage and praise good expression. Emphasise the need to check that the text makes sense to them, particularly as they tackle unfamiliar or difficult words.

REVISIT AND RESPOND

Bring the group back together and discuss some of the points below.

Note: Since there are only 20 minutes for each session, you are advised to focus on only one or two of the elements that are listed below.

- Ask the children to look at spread 7, in which the giraffe is approaching Handa. Ask: *Is the giraffe a lot taller than Handa? How does the illustrator show this? Wouldn't Handa hear the animals approaching through the grass?*
- Look at spread 9. Ask: *What is left in the basket when the parrot has stolen the passion fruit? Does Handa know what has happened?* Look back through the illustrations to find clues. *Why might Handa be suspicious?* (The basket is getting lighter and lighter.)

- Talk about adjectives. Encourage the children to identify the adjectives used in these spreads ('spiky-leaved', 'creamy green', 'tangy purple'). Then look at the descriptions of the fruit on previous pages and identify the adjectives used there ('soft yellow', 'sweet-smelling', 'round juicy', 'ripe red'). Ask the children to think of more adjectives that you could use in each case. (For example: 'curvy banana', 'yellow guava', and so on.)
- Ask the children to identify all the animals that have been illustrated so far (you could also refer to the labelled illustrations at the back of the book). Ask them if there are any animals there that they don't recognise. Talk about the different physical characteristics of the animals. Ask pairs to work together to come up with adjectives that could be used to describe each one. (For example: 'enormous grey elephant', 'tall, graceful giraffe', and so on.)
- Encourage the children to look carefully at the background illustrations for details. Discuss how these details link the scenes together. (The author gives us a reminder of what has just happened and a clue as to what will happen next.)
- Look at spread 10, where the goat appears, and ask the children to tell you what is happening in the pictures. Do they think Handa would know that something has fallen into her basket? (She would feel the bumps and it would get heavy, plus the tangerines that do not land in her basket would make a noise as they hit the ground.) Does she appear to know? What might have happened to Handa if the tree had not been there? How does she keep the basket balanced on her head with so many tangerines falling into it?
- Draw attention to the layout of the illustrations on spread 10. On the left-hand side, three panels show the goat breaking his tether and running towards Handa. Point out that the effect resembles a comic strip, or even a moving picture. Ask: *Why do you think the author has decided to do this?* (Perhaps to give an impression of how quickly the goat is moving.)

Ask the children, whenever appropriate, to revisit the text to support their answers. Encourage the children to read aloud back to the group when referring back to the text – praise clear, confident and expressive reading.

ASSESSMENT OPPORTUNITIES

The following bank of question prompts provides a quick and easy means of monitoring the children's comprehension skills and understanding of the text. The children's answers to a question must be supported by evidence from the text.

Understanding

- Who is the next to steal fruit after the giraffe?
- Who chooses the pineapple from the basket?
- What is the purple fruit in Handa's basket?
- What does the goat do when the rope snaps? Is there anything or anyone else in the field when this happens?

Inferences

- How can a giraffe pick up something as heavy and spiky as a pineapple with just its tongue?
- Why might Handa be suspicious that something has changed since she set out for Akeyo's village?
- Is Handa near her friend's house as the tangerines fall into the basket? How do you know that?
- Do you think Akeyo lives near Handa's village? Explain why you think that.
- Do you think that Handa has walked to visit Akeyo before with fruit?
- Do you think the goat is friendly? What are the clues that suggest this?
- What do you think might have happened to Handa if the tangerine tree had not been there?

Predicting

- Will Handa be surprised when she takes the basket off her head?
- Do you think Akeyo will be pleased to see her?
- Do you think Akeyo will like the fruit Handa has brought her?

Main ideas

- Do you think Handa is aware of the giraffe as it reaches for the pineapple? Why do you say that?
- Who steals the last of the fruit?
- Which fruit would you most like to try from Handa's basket from the author's description of it?

Language, structure and presentation

- Which fruit has sharp pointed leaves? How is it described in the story?
- The parrot takes the 'tangy purple passion-fruit'. Suggest another word for 'tangy'.
- Do you think the avocado is soft inside or crunchy? Which word in the story tells you that?

Themes and conventions

- Does Handa really know what is happening to her on her journey? Why or why not?

▼ SESSION 4: HANDA'S SURPRISE

SESSION AIMS

Link what they read or hear read to their own experiences.

READ

- Ask the children to read spreads 11 and 12 independently, while considering these questions.
  - Look for differences and similarities between Handa's village and Akeyo's.
  - Why are the tangerines a surprise for Akeyo? Why are they a surprise for Handa?
  - Do both girls like the surprise? Why?
  - Look at the final illustration. What are the girls laughing about?

During reading

- Move around the group and 'tune in' to hear individuals read aloud. Encourage and praise good expression. Emphasise the need to check that the text makes sense to them, particularly as they tackle unfamiliar or difficult words.

REVISIT AND RESPOND

Bring the group back together and discuss some of the points below.

Note: Since there are only 20 minutes for each session, you are advised to focus on only one or two of the elements that are listed below.

- Compare these two spreads with the first two in the book. Talk about differences and similarities between Handa's village and Akeyo's. Ask: *Can you see someone else carrying a heavy load on their head in Akeyo's village?* Encourage children to explain the differences between where Handa and Akeyo live and their own street. (For example, are there chickens in the road, do people carry things on their heads, and so on.)

- Ask the children whether they think Akeyo is expecting Handa's visit, from her reaction to her friend's arrival. Ask: *How do the two greet each other?* (Waving hands, smiling, Akeyo running towards Handa.) Ask the children if this is how they greet their friends when they visit.

- Ask: *Is Handa upset that her seven different fruits have disappeared?* (The smiles and the sharing of the tangerines suggest that both girls are happy.) Discuss whether the children have ever felt very disappointed when something has not gone as they had hoped. How did they deal with that?

- Look at how italics and capital letters are used on the final spread. Explore how this changes the way we read the words. (Akeyo's cry of 'Tangerines!' has an exclamation mark to show her surprise and delight; Handa's words are emphasised more, being in capitals with a question mark to show her greater surprise and disbelief. The word 'is' is italicised in Handa's exclamation – 'That *is* a surprise!' to show that she knew there was going to be a surprise but wasn't expecting to be surprised herself.)

- Ask the children what they think might happen on Handa's return walk home. Ask: *Will the animals come out to see her again, or will they stay away if she has no fruit to offer?*

- Look at the final illustration. Ask the children: *What are the girls laughing about? How can you tell they are laughing?* (The shape of their mouths, their heads tilted slightly backwards and their expressions look happy.)

- Read through the whole story from beginning to end with the group and encourage them to join in. Ask: *Did you enjoy the story? What was your favourite part, and why? If you could change the story at all, what would you do differently?*

- Ask the children to think about the title. Ask: *Is it a good title? What does it mean? Can you explain what Handa's surprise was?* (They could say, for example, that the surprise was meant to be Akeyo's but, in the end, it was Handa who was more surprised.)

Ask the children, whenever appropriate, to revisit the text to support their answers. Encourage them to read aloud back to the group when referring back to the text – praise clear, confident and expressive reading.

ASSESSMENT OPPORTUNITIES

The following bank of question prompts provides a quick and easy means of monitoring the children's comprehension skills and understanding of the text. The children's answers to a question must be supported by evidence from the text.

Understanding

- What does Handa say to Akeyo when she first sees her friend?
- What is Handa carrying in her basket?
- Who says tangerines are their favourite fruit?
- Give an example of an animal that lives in the villages.

Inferences

- Do you think Handa knew beforehand that her friend liked tangerines? Explain how you know that.
- Do you think Akeyo feels excited to see her friend? How do you know?
- Why do you think the girls are laughing at the end?
- Do the women work hard in Akeyo's village? Explain why you think that.
- How are the women able to work if they have children to look after? Use clues in the picture to help you explain.

Predicting

- Will Handa and Akeyo enjoy eating the tangerines?
- Do you think they will share the fruit with the other people in the village?
- How long will Handa stay in Akeyo's village before she walks home?

Main ideas

- Why are the tangerines a surprise for Akeyo? Why are they a surprise for Handa? Do both girls like the surprise? Why?
- Did you enjoy the surprise at the end of the story? Explain how it made you feel.
- What did you think of the story as a whole? Describe your favourite moment.

Language, structure and presentation

- Look at the exclamation marks on the last page. What effect do they have?
- On the last page, Handa's words include capital letters and italics. Why do you think the author has done this?
- Do you think the author chose a good title for the story? Explain why.

Themes and conventions

- How is the theme of friendship shown through the book? (Handa wants to bring her friend Akeyo a gift she will like and puts lots of thought into it.)

▼ SESSION 1: HIP, HIP, HOORAY FOR SUPERWORM

SESSION AIMS

Discuss the significance of the title and events.

READ

- Ask the children to explore the cover and read the first four spreads independently. Invite them to consider some of these questions.
  - Does the title give a clue about the story's main character? What events also helped you to decide?
  - Why do you think this ordinary-looking worm is called 'Superworm'?
  - Who do you think are Superworm's friends?
  - What do you think Superworm might do next?

During reading

- As the group read, listen to individual readers. Give praise for clear, expressive reading and to those who tackle unfamiliar or difficult words confidently.

REVISIT AND RESPOND

Bring the group back together and discuss some of the points below.

Note: Since there are only 20 minutes for each session, you are advised to focus on only one or two of the elements that are listed below.

- Read the title on the front cover and the text on the back cover together. Ask: *What do you think the title tells us about who the story is about? Can you find words that tell us Superworm is a superhero? Who is the author? Does knowing this give you a clue about how the book might be written?* (Probably in rhyme.) Re-read the rhyming chant on the back cover and agree that this might mean that the text will rhyme. Focus on the back cover quotes and help children to understand what they mean. Having explored the cover, ask: *What do you expect this book will be like?* (Funny, rhyming, fantasy, magic.)

- Before reading, discuss the concept of a superhero. Refer to their powers and the way they help the vulnerable and fight evil. Ask: *What is a superhero? What sort of powers does a superhero have? Does Superworm look like a superhero? Does he have a special costume?*

- Recall previous Julia Donaldson books and the pleasure of reading in rhyme. Read the repeated chant together and focus on how the chant appears on spread 4. Ask: *Why do these words have inverted commas when they are repeated on this page? Which words in the lines above tell us who is saying them, and how?* (Small creatures 'clap', 'cheer' and 'chant'.) Have fun pretending to be the creatures chanting, clapping and cheering. Ask: *Do you think the chant sounds more effective now? What have you added since you read it the first time?* (clapping, cheering)

- Discuss Superworm's powers. What clues about his powers can the children find in the chant? ('super-long', 'super-strong'.) Ask: *How many new 'superpower' words can you make in this way?* (For example: super-speedy, super-elastic, and so on.)

- Explore the illustrations together. Ask: *How many wild creatures can you name? Can you describe the things that are growing? What is the well for? Are there any roads? How do you know this?*

- Discuss the meaning of any new words, such as 'major', 'lasso', 'squirm' and 'disaster', and ask questions to ensure children understand them in context. For example: *How did turning into a lasso help Superworm prevent a disaster?*

- Discuss the expression 'feeling bored' on spread 2. Encourage the group to talk about times when they have been bored and how that felt. Ask: *What do you think 'no need to mope' means?* Talk about how we sometimes 'mope' around and say we are 'fed up', and move slowly because we feel 'down'. Suggest that knowing this might give us a clue about the mood of the bees, and why they needed to 'Cheer up'! Try to think of different words together to describe the bees' mood.

- Discuss the punctuation, referring to use of capitals and exclamation marks in general. Draw attention to the ellipsis at the end of spread 2. Ask the children to read the four words preceding it and then pause to think what might be on the next page. Turn over and ask: *Did you predict what would come next? How are the bees feeling now? How has Superworm used his powers to cheer them up?* Follow the same procedure with the ellipsis after the words 'all is fine…' on spread 3.

Ask the children, whenever appropriate, to revisit the text to provide evidence for their answers. Encourage them to read aloud when referring back to the text. Praise suggestions about the significance of the title and setting.

ASSESSMENT OPPORTUNITIES

The following bank of question prompts provides a quick and easy means of monitoring the children's comprehension skills and understanding of the text. The children's answers to a question must be supported by evidence from the text.

Understanding

- How does Superworm come to the rescue of the baby toad and the beetle?
- How does Superworm cheer up the bored bees?
- What is a 'major' road?

Inferences

- How do you know Superworm is 'super-strong'? (He lifts a huge stone with his tail.)
- What do you know about where the story is set?
- How do you think the other creatures feel about Superworm?

Predicting

- How could baby toad running into the major road become a 'disaster'?
- What do you think the next section will be about?

Main ideas

- How do you know that this story is written like a poem?
- What extra information did the illustrations add to the story?

Language, structure and presentation

- Can you describe the patterns in the way the words are organised?
- Why is 'SUPERWORM' written in capital letters in the creatures' chant? Why are there so many exclamation marks in the last two lines?
- Which two words has the author joined to the word 'super' to describe Superworm's powers? ('strong'/'long'.)
- Who is the book illustrator? What do you recognise about his style?

Themes and conventions

- Can you describe the type of story this is from what you have read so far? What makes you think this?
- What is different about Superworm compared to the usual superheroes?

▼ SESSION 2: WIZARD LIZARD ATTACKS

SESSION AIMS

Predict what might happen on the basis of what has been read so far.

READ

- Ask the children to read the next four spreads (5, 6, 7 and 8) independently. Invite them to consider some of these questions.
  - How does Wizard Lizard know that Superworm is near?
  - What does a servant do? Can you describe the servant crow and the job he has?
  - What sort of treasure do you think Wizard Lizard expected Superworm to find? What did he actually find?
  - What makes the creatures decide to hatch a cunning plan?

During reading

- As the group read, focus on individual readers. Give praise for clear, expressive reading and to those who are already making predictions about what will happen next.

REVISIT AND RESPOND

Bring the group back together and discuss some of the points below.

Note: Since there are only 20 minutes for each session, you are advised to focus on only one or two of the elements that are listed below.

- Focus on the introduction of the new evil character, Wizard Lizard, and the children's experience of stories involving good triumphing over evil. Ask: *Who do you think the hero and villain are going to be in this story? What sort of character is Wizard Lizard? How do you know that he can do magic? Where does the magic power come from? Can you predict what sort of magic he will do?*

- Focus on the vocabulary to ensure that children fully understand the text. Discuss the meaning of 'servant' and 'boss'. Ask: *What does a servant do? What did Wizard Lizard ask his servant crow to do? Can you describe what a 'boss' does? Why is Superworm cross to have Wizard Lizard as a boss? How do you think a boss should behave? Do you think Wizard Lizard will behave in this way?* Discuss the meaning of the word 'hatch' in the context of giving birth and then link this to the word 'plan'. Talk about how the creatures are inventing or 'giving birth to' a new plan, and why it needs to be 'cunning'. Link 'cunning' to the behaviour of a fox in stories, and suggest that the creatures must behave in this way to outwit the lizard. Discuss the word 'lair' and the kind of creature who lives in one.

- Recall the superpowers that Superworm has and discuss what happens to make him lose them. Ask: *What does Wizard Lizard mean when he says 'you're in my power'? Did you predict that Wizard Lizard would overpower Superworm? What happens to Superworm under Wizard Lizard's power? Why is he unable to use his own power? What does Wizard Lizard make him do?*

- Compare the meaning of the movement words Wizard Lizard uses to describe how he wants Superworm to tunnel in the soil ('writhe' and 'coil') with the words that describe how he actually moves ('twists' and 'winds'). Ask questions to ensure the children understand the difference between these words in context. For example: *Why do you think Wizard Lizard chose the words 'writhe' and 'coil' to describe Superworm's movements in the soil? Can you demonstrate how someone would move if they had a bad pain, and how they would move if they were not in pain? Why do you think Wizard Lizard wanted Superworm to suffer?*

- Focus on the reaction of the creatures when they discover that their hero is in trouble. Encourage the children to predict what might happen next based on the way the creatures feel about their hero.

Ask the children to revisit the text to provide evidence for their answers. Encourage them to read aloud when referring back to the text. Praise evidence of clear understanding of the text and appropriate predictions about the consequences of actions.

ASSESSMENT OPPORTUNITIES

The following bank of question prompts provides a quick and easy means of monitoring the children's comprehension skills and understanding of the text. The children's answers to a question must be supported by evidence from the text.

Understanding

- Where does Wizard Lizard live?
- What is Wizard Lizard going to do with Superworm if he fails to find the treasure?
- What does Superworm actually find in the soil? How does Wizard Lizard react?
- How do the creatures know that the servant crow is excited about eating Superworm?

Inferences

- What do you think are the qualities of a good boss? Do you think Wizard Lizard is a good boss?
- How do you think the creatures feel when the servant crow flies past with Superworm in his beak?
- How is Superworm feeling as he tries to 'slink' away from Wizard Lizard? Which word tells you this?

Predicting

- Do you think Superworm will find some real treasure for Wizard Lizard? What makes you say this?
- What do you think will happen in the next part of the story?

Main ideas

- What do you understand by a 'lair'? What creatures do you know that have lairs?
- What effect does the magic flower have on Superworm?
- Can you name the creatures involved in hatching a cunning plan?

Language, structure and presentation

- Which word has been shortened with an apostrophe to create the contraction 'He'll'? Which two letters have been removed?
- What is meant by 'At the double'/'Hatch a cunning plan'? Why does the author use these phrases?

Themes and conventions

- Can you describe the hero and villain in another story you have read? How did good triumph over evil?
- How do you know this story has magic in it?

▼ SESSION 3: THE CUNNING PLAN

Link what they read or listen to with their own experiences.

READ

- Ask the children to read the next four spreads (9 to 12) independently, bearing in mind some of these questions.
  - Can you describe the scene when the creatures enter Wizard Lizard's lair?
  - How do the creatures capture Wizard Lizard?
  - Why do you think they choose to use a honeycomb, leaves and a web?
  - How does the magic flower lose its power?

During reading

- As the group read together, listen to individuals. Praise those who quote their own experiences to demonstrate understanding of the content.

REVISIT AND RESPOND

Bring the group back together and discuss some of the points below.

Note: Since there are only 20 minutes for each session, you are advised to focus on only one or two of the elements that are listed below.

- Focus on the teamwork displayed by the creatures as they carry out their plan. Talk about the different roles the friends play, and encourage children to make links with their own experiences of working as a team, perhaps during a school project or in a game. Ask: *Why do you think the creatures want to help Superworm? What is so special about him? How do they work together to capture the wizard? What do the snails/beetles/bees do? Who fetches the leaves? What does the spider do? Have you ever worked as a team? What part did you play? Have you ever had a problem and been helped to solve it by your friends?*

- Discuss the feelings of Wizard Lizard now that he is the victim instead of the captor. Ask: *How do you think Wizard Lizard feels when he wakes up to find himself trapped? Do you think he feels the same as Superworm did when he could not escape? Have you ever felt really scared? Can you describe what happened to you?*

- Focus on the movement words on spread 9. Ask children to say which creatures 'jump', which 'fly', which 'crawl' and which ones 'creep'. Encourage them to think of words to describe the way slugs and snails move.

- Explore the spread depicting Wizard Lizard being dumped into the rubbish. Read the text on the left-hand page and discuss how the punctuation creates dramatic effect. Ask: *Why do you think the reader is invited to pause after the word 'and…' before reading the words BANG! CRASH! THUMP! Why do you think these words are in capital letters? Why are there exclamation marks after these words and at the end of the final sentence?* Now ask the children to read the text on this page again with appropriate expression, adding claps or stamps if they wish to.

- Discuss the way illustrations enhance this section; for example, as the creatures jump, fly, crawl and creep along with the honeycomb. Talk about how we know exactly who carries it, and how, and how we can see how sticky it is from the drips coming from it. Explore the gloomy, spooky image of the wizard's lair, with fireflies lighting it, and the clever way the caterpillars carry leaves stuck to the bristles on their backs. Discuss the expression on Wizard Lizard's face and the desperate clawing of his feet when trapped in the web. Ask: *Which is your favourite illustration? Why do you like it? What extra information do you think it gives to the reader?*

Ask the children to explore the text in detail to provide evidence for their answers, and encourage them to read aloud when referring back to it. Comment on expressive reading and praise those who mention experiences of their own when demonstrating their understanding of the text.

ASSESSMENT OPPORTUNITIES

The following bank of question prompts provides a quick and easy means of monitoring the children's comprehension skills and understanding of the text. The children's answers to a question must be supported by evidence from the text.

Understanding

- How important do you think teamwork is? Can you explain why you think this?
- Why do you think Wizard Lizard is unable to use magic to escape from the web?
- If you could ask Wizard Lizard a question linked to what happens to him, what would it be?

Inferences

- Can you suggest a cunning plan to capture Wizard Lizard? Who would help you?
- Why do you think the friends drop Wizard Lizard in the rubbish dump?
- Do you think the flies lighting up the wizard's lair are fireflies? Why will they be useful to the other creatures?

Predicting

- Do you think the bird looking down on Wizard Lizard in the rubbish is his servant crow? Do you think he might try to help or simply ignore him? Why do you think this?
- What do you think is causing the 'distant rumbling sound' in the earth?
- Why do you think the ellipsis invites you to pause before turning over spread 12? What do you think will happen next?

Main ideas

- Why do you think Wizard Lizard holds his magic flower while he sleeps?
- Do you think Superworm will return before the story ends? Why do you think this?

Language, structure and presentation

- Which adjective describing the creatures on spread 9 also explains more about the setting? ('garden'.)
- Which words does the author use to describe the web to show that Wizard Lizard will not be able to escape from it?
- Which letters has the author added to the adjective 'busy' to change it into an adverb that describes how the spider weaves the web?
- Why do you think there is an ellipsis after the word 'creep' on spread 9 and before the word 'and' on spread 10?

Themes and conventions

- Do you enjoy reading stories in rhyme? What is your favourite rhyme from this section?
- How do you think a wizard speaks? Read Wizard Lizard's words in this section in your 'wizard voice'.

▼ SESSION 4: SUPERWORM IS BACK AGAIN!

SESSION AIMS

Recognise and join in with predictable phrases.

READ

- Ask the children to read the final three spreads independently. Invite them to consider some of these questions.
  - What is the big surprise for the creatures at the start of this section?
  - Where do you think Superworm has been while the creatures have been capturing Wizard Lizard?
  - How does Superworm amuse his friends on his return?
  - Do you think this is a good ending to the story? Why do you think this?

During reading

- As the group read together, listen to individuals and praise their expression and clarity. Comment positively to those who repeat the chant with confidence.

REVISIT AND RESPOND

Bring the group back together and discuss some of the points below.

Note: Since there are only 20 minutes for each session, you are advised to focus on only one or two of the elements that are listed below.

- Explore the spread depicting Superworm transforming into amusing creations. Discuss the importance of the illustrations and comment on the extra information they provide. Ask: *Does seeing the props Superworm uses as an acrobat and a slide help you to imagine this in greater detail?* Point out that on this spread the text resembles labels alongside individual illustrations. Compare this with the final spread where there is one large illustration, with the text displayed like a poem alongside. Ask: *Do you prefer small individual illustrations or one large one? Why do you like this? Can you describe the rhyming pattern of the 'labels' on the smaller*

illustrations? How does this compare with the pattern on the last page? Which rhyming pattern do you prefer? Why do you think there is an exclamation mark at the end of each label?

- Explore the expressions of the creatures on the first and last spreads of this section and notice how they change from shock and disbelief to joy and delight once they realise their friend is really back again. Ask: *Why do you think the friends look shocked when Superworm appears from the soil? What does Superworm do to make them confident that he is back again? How do they demonstrate their joy on the last page?*

- Focus on the chant on the last page and ask the group to recall where they have read it before. Identify that it forms the first and last lines in the book and discuss the importance of this. If necessary, pose the notion that the chant introduces Superworm at the beginning, and the friends take over the chant to create a satisfying end. Consider whether this repetition emphasises the importance of the main character. Ask: *Who do you think is speaking? Do you like the way the chant is repeated at these important points in the book, and why?*

- Ask in what context the children have heard the whole of the last spread before. (On spread 4.) Discuss aspects of the text that help us to remember it, such as repetition, memorable rhyming words and a strong rhythm. Read the first 'verse' and suggest switching words around, saying 'sister slugs and brother snails' instead of the other way round. Try repeating the words with these changes and ask: *Do you think the words sound as satisfying now? What has happened to the rhythm? Are they as easy to remember?*

- Ask the group to repeat the four lines the creatures chant on the final spread without looking at the book. Discuss how emphasising the rhythm helps and suggest clapping quietly and steadily to emphasise the beats. Finally, ask the children to choose a creature to imitate and to chant in this voice. Talk about the fun of speaking in rhyme, in character and in unison.

Ask the children to look for evidence for their answers in the text, and encourage them to read this evidence aloud to the group. Praise clear, expressive reading and positively encourage those who join in with the predictable phrases.

ASSESSMENT OPPORTUNITIES

The following bank of question prompts provides a quick and easy means of monitoring the children's comprehension skills and understanding of the text. The children's answers to a question must be supported by evidence from the text.

Understanding

- Which of Superworm's creations in this section is your favourite? Can you describe how it works?
- If you could ask Superworm a question linked to the final three spreads, what would it be?

Inferences

- What do you think the creatures thought had happened to Superworm?
- How do you think the creatures feel when their friend first emerges from the soil?

Predicting

- If you were Superworm, how would you amuse your friends? What would you turn into?
- If you were writing a sequel to this story, what would happen to Superworm and his friends?
- Do you think Superworm and his friends will ever meet Wizard Lizard again?

Main ideas

- What does this story tell us about the importance of friendship?
- Would you say Superworm is a true superhero? Why do you think this?

Language, structure and presentation

- Why do you think 'SUPERWORM' is in capital letters and all of the letters are larger on the first page of this section?
- What do you like about how the page showing the things that Superworm transforms into to amuse his friends is presented?
- Can you choose three illustrations you particularly like and describe how they add detail to the text?

Themes and conventions

- Do you think this story has a satisfying beginning and end? Can you say why?
- Do you think this story has all of these elements – humour, fantasy and magic? Can you give examples of each?

▼ GUIDED READING RECORD

Year		Term	
Group		Reading target	

Date	Text	Objectives	Names	Comments

Notes

M SCHOLASTIC

READ & RESPOND

Bringing the best books to life in the classroom

BOOK:

· ·

· ·

· ·

· ·

· ·

· ·

· ·

· ·

· ·

· ·

· ·

M SCHOLASTIC

READ & RESPOND

Bringing the best books to life in the classroom

BOOK:

· ·

· ·

· ·

· ·

· ·

· ·

· ·

· ·

· ·

· ·

· ·

READ & RESPOND

Bringing the best books to life in the classroom

Plan with confidence

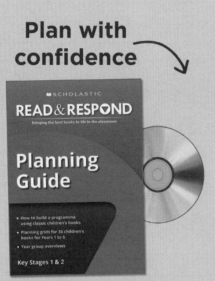

The Planning Guide provides a teaching structure for Years 1–6.

Boost guided reading time

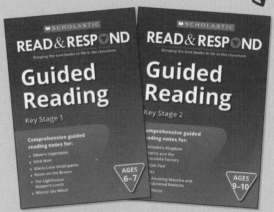

Six guided reading books are available, for Years 1–6.

Teach the best children's books

A huge range of Teacher's Books are available for Years 1–6.

Engage every reader

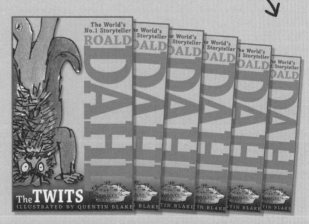

Children's books are available in sets of 6 and 30.

Order at www.scholastic.co.uk/readandrespond
or call us on 0845 6039091